CONTENTS

3

Layout by Günter Beer & Sigurd Buchberger
(www.webdesignindex.org)
Cover and book design by Pepin van Roojen
CD Master by Sigurd Buchberger

Introduction by Günter Beer and Pepin van Roojen

With special thanks to Magda Garcia Masana, Justyna
Wrzodak, Weihong Liu, Michie Yamakawa and Vladimir
Nazarov.

Web Design Index 7
ISBN 978 90 5768 105 9
The Pepin Press | Agile Rabbit Editions
Amsterdam & Singapore

The Pepin Press BV
P.O. Box 10349
1001 EH Amsterdam
The Netherlands

Tel +31 20 4202021
Fax +31 20 4201152
mail@pepinpress.com
www.pepinpress.com

10 9 8 7 6 5 4 3 2 1
2011   2010   2009   2008   2007

Manufactured in Singapore

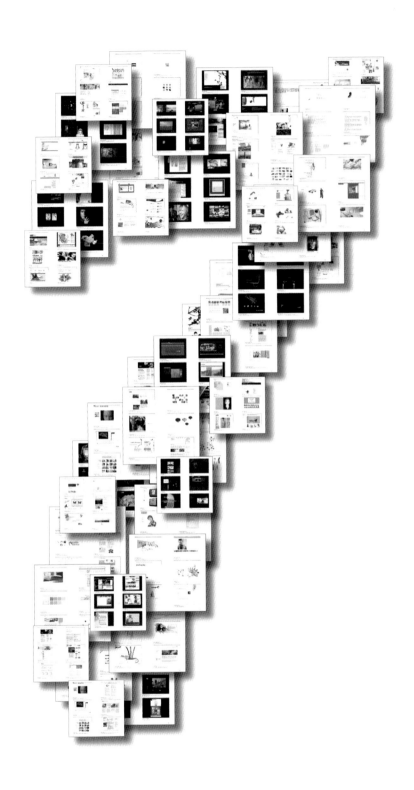

Compiled & Edited by Günter Beer

THE PEPIN PRESS | AGILE RABBIT EDITIONS
AMSTERDAM & SINGAPORE

For many types of communication, websites have replaced printed media as the main tool. In other instances, Internet applications have gained an important position next to traditional media. Use of the Internet has reached a stage of maturity, and the same can be said of web design: over the past ten years, it has changed from hesitant and experimental to confident and sophisticated. The increasingly common use of fast-speed Internet allows designers to use larger image files, and it has become more common for clients to allocate a budget for professional photography.

The captions in this book provide information about those involved in the design and programming and are coded as follows:

D   design
C   coding
P   production
A   agency
M   designer's contact address

A CD-ROM containing all the pages, arranged in the same order as the book, can be found inside the back cover. It allows you to view each page on your computer with a minimum of loading time, and to access the Internet in order to browse the selected pages.

Submissions & recommendations

Each year, brand new editions of all The Pepin Press' web design books are published. Should you wish to submit or recommend designs for consideration, please access the submissions form at www.webdesignindex.org.

The Pepin Press/Agile Rabbit Editions

For more information about The Pepin Press' many publications on design, fashion, popular culture, visual reference and ready-to-use images, please visit www.pepinpress.com.

多くのコミュニケーション分野で、印刷媒体に取って代わってウェブサイトが、主なツールになってきました。インターネット・アプリケーションが従来のメディアに次いで重要な位置を占めるようになった分野もあります。インターネットは成熟期に入りました。ウェブデザインについても同じです。この10年間で、ウェブデザインは、実験的に試行錯誤をしていた段階から、洗練されて、自信に満ちあふれたものに変わってきました。高速インターネットの普及で、デザイナーが使えるイメージ・ファイルのサイズは大きくなり、プロ・レベルのハイクオリティの写真も手頃な予算で使えるようになりました。

この本のキャプションで使用されている略字の意味は、以下のとおりです。

D　　　デザイン
C　　　コーディング
P　　　プロダクション
A　　　エージェンシー
M　　　デザイナーの連絡先

裏表紙の内側ポケットに挿入されたCD-ROMには、同書の全ページがページ順に収録されています。このCD-ROMをお客様のコンピューターでご使用になれば、各ページを簡単に見ることができます。また、同書に掲載されているウェブ・ページにも、簡単にアクセスできます。

応募及び推薦について

ザ・ペピン・プレス発行のウェブデザイン関連の本は毎年改訂されています。デザイン掲載をご希望の方は、あるいは掲載にふさわしいと思われるデザインを推薦なさりたい場合は、以下のアドレスにアクセスし、所定の応募フォームをご使用ください。
www.webdesignindex.org

ザ・ペピン・プレス／アジャイレ・ラビット・エディションズ

ザ・ペピン・プレスはデザインやファッション、ポップ・カルチャー、ビジュアル参考書、すぐに使用可能なイメージを収録した書籍を出版しております。弊社商品について、もっと詳しいことをお知りになりたい方は、以下の弊社サイトにアクセスしてください。
www.pepinpress.com

在各类信息传达方式中，网站已经取代打印媒介成为了主要的手段。在其它情形下，互联网应用已经取得了同传统媒介不相上下的重要地位。无论如何，互联网的使用已经进入了成熟的阶段，而网页设计亦复如此：在过去十年，它已经从迟疑和实验阶段走向了充满自信的阶段。

本书的标题提供了关于涉足设计和编程的人员的信息，并确定编码如下：

D   设计
C   编码
P   制作
A   代理
M   设计人员的联系地址

CD光盘放在封底，它包含所有的网页，并按照本书的顺序进行排列。光盘可以让你利用你自己的计算机，在最短的加载时间内对各个网页进行阅览，并登录互联网浏览精选的网页。

提交及推荐

Pepin出版社每年都发行网页设计册的新版本。如果你希望提交或推荐任何设计以供考虑，请登录www.webdesignindex.org上的提交表。

Pepin 出版社/Agile Rabbit 版本

关于Pepin出版社在设计，时尚，大众文化，虚拟参考和备用图片方面的众多出版物的更多详细信息，请访问www.pepinpress.com

网页设计索引 中文

다양한 형태의 의사전달 방식에 있어서, 웹사이트는 주요 수단으로서 인쇄 매체를 대신하였습니다.

다른 경우에서도, 인터넷의 사용은 전통적인 매체 다음으로 중요한 위치를 차지하게 되었습니다.

어떤 이유로서든지, 이제 인터넷은 완숙한 단계에 접어들었고, 동시에 웹디자인도 마찬가지의 상황이 되었습니다. 즉, 지난 십여 년 동안 웹디자인은 생소하고 실험적인 단계로부터 확신할 수 있고 더욱 정교한 차원으로 변화되어 왔습니다.

나날이 보편화 되는 고속 인터넷 사용은 디자이너로 하여금 더 큰 이미지 파일을 사용할 수 있게 하였고 고객을 위하여 전문가적인 사진기술에 예산을 할당하는 것은 이제 더욱 일반적인 현상이 되었습니다.

이 책에서의 캡션 설명은 디자인과 프로그래밍에 관한 내용을 제공하고 있으며 아래와 같은 코드로 표시하고 있습니다.

D   디자인
C   코딩
P   제작
A   대행사
M   디자이너 연락처

모든 페이지가 수록된 CD는 책에 수록된 순서와 같은 순서로 배열되어 있으며, 책 뒤의 덮개 안에 부착되어 있습니다.

사용자는 자신의 컴퓨터에서 최소의 로딩 시간으로 각각의 페이지를 볼 수 있으며, 선택한 페이지를 찾고자 인터넷에 접속할 수도 있습니다.

신청과 추천
매년, 페핀 프레스(Pepin Press)는 웹디자인의 신간 서적을 출판합니다. 신청을 원하시거나 검토를 위해 디자인 추천을 원하시면, 웹사이트 www.webdesignindex.org로 신청양식을 접속하시기 바랍니다.

The Pepin Press / Agile Rabbit Editions 페핀 프레스 / 애절 래빗 에디션즈
페핀 프레스의 다양한 서적 – 디자인, 패션, 유행문화, 비주얼 레퍼런스 및 즉시사용 이미지 등에 관한 자세한 안내는 www.pepinpress.com을 방문하여주십시오.

In zahlreichen Kommunikationsbereichen hat die Website das Printmedium als wichtigstes Werkzeug verdrängt, oder zumindest eine Position eingenommen, die in ihrer Bedeutung den traditionellen Medien gleichkommt. Inzwischen ist das Internet (und seine Nutzung) den Kinderschuhen entwachsen – was gleichermaßen für das Webdesign gilt: Im Laufe der vergangenen zehn Jahre hat in diesem Bereich eine Entwicklung vom zögerlichen und experimentellen Gebrauch hin zur sicheren und selbstverständlichen Verwendung stattgefunden.

Die Bildunterschriften in diesem Buch enthalten wichtige Angaben zu den für Design und Programmierung Verantwortlichen. Dabei wurden folgende Codes verwendet:

D   Design
C   Code
P   Produktion
A   Agentur
M   Kontaktadresse

In der hinteren Umschlagseite befindet sich eine CD-ROM mit allen abgebildeten Webseiten. Die Reihenfolge entspricht der Anordnung im Buch. So können Sie mit minimaler Ladezeit jede Seite auf dem Bildschirm betrachten oder die ausgewählten Seiten im Internet aufrufen.

Vorschläge und Empfehlungen
Pepin Press bringt jedes Jahr eine neue Ausgabe seiner Bücher zum Thema Webdesign heraus. Wenn Sie eine Website für unsere zukünftigen Publikationen vorschlagen oder empfehlen möchten, verwenden Sie bitte das entsprechende Formular auf www.webdesignindex.org

The Pepin Press / Agile Rabbit Editions
Weitere Informationen zu den zahlreichen Veröffentlichungen von Pepin Press - in den Bereichen Design, Mode und Popkultur, mit visuellem Referenzmaterial und sofort verwendbaren Bildern für Designer - finden Sie auf unserer Website www.pepinpress.com

Per tanti tipi di comunicazione, i siti web hanno sostituito i media stampati quale strumento centrale. In altri casi, le applicazioni internet hanno guadagnato una posizione di rilievo a fianco ai media tradizionali. In ogni caso, l'uso di internet ha raggiunto una fase di maturità, e la stessa affermazione si applica al web design: nel corso degli ultimi dieci anni, è cambiato da esitante e sperimentale a fiducioso e sofisticato. L'uso sempre più comune di internet a banda larga permette ai disegners di utilizzare file d'immagine più grandi e sta diventando più comune per i clienti di allocare un budget alla fotografia professionale.

Le intestazioni in questo libro forniscono informazioni su coloro che sono coinvolti nel design e nella programmazione, e sono codificati secondo lo schema seguente:

D   desgin
C   codificazione
P   produzione
A   agenzia
M   contatti del designer

Un CD ROM contenente tutte le pagine, collocate nella stessa maniera che nel libro, si trovano all'interno della copertina posteriore. Permette di visualizzare ogni pagina sul vostro computer con un tempo di scaricamento minimo, e di accedere a internet in modo da sfogliare le pagine selezionate.

Consegne & raccomandazioni

Tutti gli anni vengono pubblicate le nuove edizioni dei libri sul web design della Pepin Press. Nel caso in cui voleste consegnare o raccomandare dei design da considerare, consultate per favore il modulo di presentazione allo www.webdesignindex.org.

The Pepin Press / Agile Rabbit Editions

Per maggiori informazioni sulle numerose pubblicazioni della Pepin Press sul design, la moda, la cultura popolare, referenze visuali e immagini pronte da utilizzare, potete consultare il sito www.pepinpress.com.

En muchos tipos de comunicación, las páginas web han sustituido a los medios impresos en su papel como herramientas primordiales. En otros casos, las aplicaciones de Internet han adquirido una posición relevante junto a los soportes tradicionales. De cualquier manera, el uso de Internet ha alcanzado su estado de madurez, y lo mismo puede decirse del diseño de páginas web: en el último decenio ha pasado de ser dubitativo y experimental a ser un diseño sofisticado y con valía propia. La difusión de las conexiones rápidas a Internet permite a los diseñadores utilizar archivos de imagen de mayor tamaño, y cada vez es más frecuente que los clientes destinen una parte del presupuesto a la fotografía profesional.

Los nombres de quienes han participado en el diseño y la programación de cada sitio se citan en los pies de foto de la siguiente manera:

D   diseño
C   codificación
P   producción
A   agencia
M   dirección de contacto del diseñador

En el interior de la contracubierta encontrará un CD-ROM que contiene todas las páginas web, ordenadas según aparecen en este libro. Si lo desea, puede verlas en su ordenador (el tiempo de carga es mínimo) y acceder a Internet para explorar en su totalidad las páginas seleccionadas.

Sugerencias y recomendaciones
La editorial The Pepin Press publica cada año ediciones actualizadas de sus libros sobre diseño de páginas web. Si desea proponernos algún diseño que considere recomendable, rellene nuestro formulario de sugerencias, que encontrará en la página web www.webdesignindex.org.

The Pepin Press/Agile Rabbit Editions
Para obtener información adicional acerca de las múltiples publicaciones de The Pepin Press en materia de diseño, moda, cultura popular, referencia visual e imágenes listas para usar, visite la página web de la editorial en www.pepinpress.com.

Em muitos tipos de comunicação, os sítios web substituíram o suporte de impressão como ferramenta principal. Noutros casos, a utilização na Internet conquistou um papel importante ao lado dos suportes tradicionais. Seja como for, a utilização da Internet atingiu o estado de maturidade e o mesmo se pode dizer do web design: durante os últimos dez anos evoluiu de hesitante e experimental para confiante e sofisticado. A utilização cada vez mais comum da Internet de alta velocidade permite que os designers utilizem ficheiros de imagem de tamanho maior e torna-se comum que os clientes atribuam um orçamento para fotografia profissional.

As legendas neste livro fornecem informações sobre todos os envolvidos no design e programação, sendo indicados do seguinte modo:

D   design
C   codificação
P   produção
A   agência
M   endereço de contacto do designer

No interior da contracapa do livro, encontrará um CD-ROM contendo todas as páginas, organizadas pela mesma ordem do livro. Este permite-lhe visualizar cada página no seu computador com um tempo de transferência mínima e aceder à Internet para navegar pelas páginas seleccionadas.

Participações e recomendações
Todos os anos são publicadas novas edições dos livros de design da Pepin Press. Se desejar enviar ou recomendar trabalhos de design para consideração, aceda ao formulário de participação em www.webdesignindex.org.

The Pepin Press / Agile Rabbit Editions
Para mais informações sobre as muitas publicações sobre design, moda, cultura popular, referência visual e imagens prontas a usar da Pepin Press, visite www.pepinpress.com.

Pour bon nombre de moyens de communication, les sites Web sont devenus le principal outil, détrônant ainsi les supports imprimés. Dans le même temps, les applications Web ont pris leur place aux côtés des médias traditionnels. Par ailleurs, l'utilisation d'Internet est parvenue à un stade de maturité, tout comme la conception Web : au cours des dix dernières années, cette discipline a franchi une étape d'incertitude et d'expérimentation pour parvenir à une place assurée et estimée. L'utilisation toujours plus répandue des accès Internet à large bande permet aux designers d'employer des fichiers image plus volumineux. D'autre part, les clients tendent de plus en plus à allouer un budget spécifique à la photographie professionnelle.

Les légendes de cet ouvrage indiquent qui a participé à la conception et à la programmation des sites. Elles sont abrégées comme suit :

D   design
C   programmation
P   production
A   agence
M   adresse du concepteur

La quatrième de couverture contient un CD-ROM présentant l'ensemble des pages Web, dans le même ordre que le livre. Il permet de charger rapidement chaque page pour les consulter à l'écran et d'accéder à Internet pour naviguer sur les sites choisis.

Candidatures et recommandations
Chaque année, de nouvelles éditions des livres de The Pepin Press sur la conception Web sont publiées. Si vous souhaitez soumettre ou recommander un site Web, veuillez remplir le formulaire de candidature que vous trouverez à l'adresse www.webdesignindex.org.

Éditions The Pepin Press / Agile Rabbit
Pour en savoir plus sur les nombreuses publications de The Pepin Press concernant le design, la mode, la culture populaire, les documents visuels de référence et les images prêtes à l'emploi, veuillez consulter www.pepinpress.com.

W przypadku wielu typów komunikacji strony internetowe zastąpiły media drukowane, a obok innych mediów tradycyjnych, aplikacje internetowe uzyskały ważną pozycję. Zarówno użycie Internetu jak i projektowanie stron internetowych osiągnęły wysoki stopień rozwoju: w przeciągu ostatniego dziesięciolecia zmieniły się z niepewnych i eksperymentalnych w pewne i wyrafinowane. Coraz bardziej powszechne użycie szybkich połączeń internetowych pozwala projektantom wykorzystywać większe pliki obrazów, a dla klientów coraz bardziej zwyczajne staje się przydzielanie budżetu na fotografię profesjonalną.

Podpisy pod obrazami zawierają dane osób zaangażowanych w projektowanie i programowanie stron internetowych. Są one podawane następująco:

D   projektowanie
C   kodowanie
P   wykonanie
A   agencja
M   adres email projektanta

Na tylnej stronie okładki znajduje się CD-ROM zawierający wszystkie strony, które ułożone są w takiej samej kolejności jak w książce. Tym sposobem możecie Państwo poprzez jedno kliknięcie przeglądać każdą stronę na Państwa ekranie lub wywoływać wybrane strony z Internetu.

Propozycje i rekomendacje
Każdego roku wydawnictwo The Pepin Press publikuje nowe edycje książek Web Design Index. Jeśli mają Państwo życzenie przedłożyć lub polecić nam projekt, proszę wypełnić odpowiedni formularz na stronie internetowej www.webdesignindex.org.

Wydawnictwo The Pepin Press / Agile Rabbit Editions
Więcej informacji o licznych publikacjach wydawnictwa The Pepin Press na temat projektowania, mody, kultury, referencji wizualnych oraz gotowych do bezpośredniego użycia obrazów znajdą Państwo na stronie internetowej www.pepinpress.com.

Во многих сферах деятельности веб-сайты уже практически вытеснили печатные издания. В других областях, Интернет-приложения завоевали важное место вслед за традиционными СМИ. В любом случае, использование Интернета достигло стадии зрелости, и то же самое мы можем сказать и о веб-дизайне: за последние десять лет он преобразился от примитивного и экспериментального к располагающему и технологичному. Возрастающее распространение высокоскоростного Интернета позволяет дизайнерам использовать более объемные файлы изображений, а заказчикам сайтов – тратить свой бюджет на прекрасные работы профессиональных фотографов.

В описании каждого сайта приводится информация о его создателях, отмеченная следующим образом:

D   дизайн
C   программирование
P   производство
A   агентство
M   контактный адрес дизайнера

В конце книги Вы найдете CD-ROM, включающий веб-страницы в той же последовательности, в которой они представлены в книге. С помощью этого диска Вы сможете рассмотреть все детали интересующих Вас веб-страниц, а также осуществить быстрый доступ в Интернет для просмотра содержания соответствующих сайтов.

Подача на рассмотрение заявок и рекомендации

Новые издания книг по веб-дизайну издательства The Pepin Press публикуются каждый год. Если вы желаете подать на рассмотрение заявку или порекомендовать какой-либо дизайн, заполните, пожалуйста, бланк заявки на сайте www.webdesignindex.org.

Издательство The Pepin Press / Agile Rabbit Editions

За дополнительной информацией об основных публикациях издательства The Pepin Press по дизайну, моде, современной культуре, визуальным справочникам и библиотекам высококачественных изображений, обращайтесь на сайт www.pepinpress.com.

.androids

www.androids.be
D: marijke jaspers C: tim verhees P: marijke jaspers
A: supertonic design M: marijke.jaspers@gmail.com

www.blaue-gans.at
D: jung von matt, vienna C: richard hudeczek P: mouse media
A: jung von matt, vienna M: richard@mouse-media.net

01	02	03	04	05	06	07	08	09	10
11	12	13	14	15	16	17	18	19	20
21	22	23	24	25	26	27	28	29	30
31	32	33	34	35	36	37	38	39	40
41	42	43	44	45	46	47	48	49	50
51	52	53	54	55	56	57	58	59	60
60	61	62	63	64	65	66	67	68	69

© IT IS MY PARTY WORKS LIST BOOK & MORE CONTACT

IT IS ONLINE PORTFOLIO OF PAUL PAPER.
ALL PHOTOS FOUND ON THIS WEBSPACE
BELONGS TO PAUL PAPER. ©
LT / EU

PUTTING A TARGET WHERE THE HEART IS SINCE TWOTHOUSANDFIVE
WEBSPACE MADE AT © IT IS BLANK ▶

www.itismyparty.org
D: jurgis griskevicius C: jurgis griskevicius
A: it is blank M: www.itisblank.com

www.calhordas.com
D: pedro calhordas
M: pedro@calhordas.com

www.sx70.dk
D: lars bregendahl bro C: lars bregendahl bro P: lars bregendahl bro
A: westend.dk M: www.westend.dk

www.plrds.com
D: mike brodie
M: brodiebike@hotmail.com

www.pocketwebsite.net
D: marcello boschetti C: marcello boschetti P: marcello boschetti
A: bosqnet M: marcello@boschetti.net

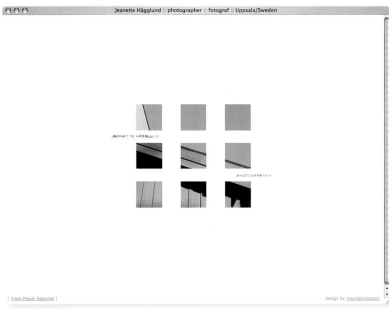

[Flash Player Required]   design by mscreativestudio

www.jeanettehagglund.com
D: santoni massimo
A: ms creative studio M: www.mscreativestudio.com

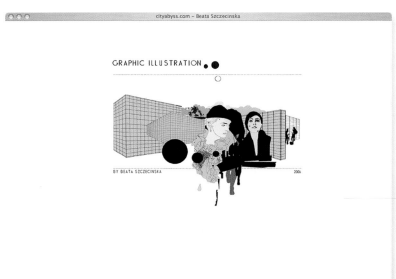

www.cityabyss.com
D: beata szczecinska C: grzegorz ogorek P: beata szczecinska
A: cityabyss M: info@cityabyss.com

"金魚すくい"は日本の祭りでよく見られるゲームです。
薄く破れ易い紙を貼った網で、
たらいの中の金魚をすくい上げます。
すくった金魚は持って帰る事が出来ます。

Kingyo-sukui is a game often seen at festivals in Japan.
People scoop up goldfish swimming in the tub
with a net made of the thin breakable paper.
They can take home the goldfish that they scooped up successfully.

about jjltd >   back >

www.jjltdskingyo.jp
D: jjltd
M: mail_to@jjltdskingyo.jp

- animation for the Shift (Germany) logo of www.shift.de - november 2005

-cover of Shift Japan, an on-line magazine about design : www.shift.jp.org ... read the article about me! - June 2005

- soon online : hidden animation for the Schloss Solitude : www.akademie-solitude.de : a landscape growing every month, with scaring surprises... keep cool!

- soon online : www.paris.com / www.parisHotels.com

- the site for "sketch" a place to be, in London : www.sketch.uk.com [see the high speed pages] - august 2004

- the web site of the fine art school of Valence [lécole régionale des beaux-arts de valence] www.erba-valence.fr see also the animation for the new year 2003 www.erba-valence.fr/bonne_annee.html - february 2003

- for christmas, "le calendrier de l'avent" for "le Pavillon" 2002-2003 (unité pédagogique du Palais de Tokyo) special low design, special for kids - december 2002

- fresh : an animation for the launching of the new web site of the production house "premiere heure" - february 2002.

- www.saison-numerique.org : web site order by the ministry of the culture of France, platform for showing themultimedia artistic scene in France, for the year 2002. This site is not anymore in line, so you just can see the empty structure I made, without content, here - september 2001

- the first web site of the Palais de Tokyo (contemporary art center in Paris) [see also the animations "Tokyoplay"] - june 2001

- see also the little site of my little village, in the Pyrénées (mountain of south France) : www.argut-dessus.com - July 2003

- contact : mail@katya-bonnenfant.com it's me! yeah! yeah!

www.katya-bonnenfant.com
D: katya bonnenfant
M: mail@katya-bonnenfant.com

iris klein

WORKS	CURRENT EXHIBITIONS	**CURRENT EXHIBITIONS**
EXHIBITIONS	UPCOMING EXHIBITIONS	PROPS & PROSTHESIS
BIOGRAPHY	ARCHIVE	REVERBERATIONS OF THE BODY IN
STATEMENT		CONTEMPORARY AUSTRIAN ART
ARTICLES / REVIEWS		
CONTACT		

CURRENT EXHIBITIONS

PROPS & PROSTHESIS
REVERBERATIONS OF THE BODY IN
CONTEMPORARY AUSTRIAN ART

Ljubljana, Jelovškova kapela in Grad Kodeljevo, October 2006

Curator: Walter Seidl
Authors: Gyula Fodor, Sabine Bitter/Helmut Weber, Markus Schinwald, Ursula Mayer, Sonja Gangl and Iris Klein.

Props & Prosthesis deals with the changing dynamic with which issues of the body, its status as a cultural signifier, and its representation as an uncanny object/subject have recently been perceived in contemporary visual arts. Focusing on the medium of photography, the exhibition questions the technical and ontological moments of this medium, whose visual output constantly oscillates between reality and fiction, between what is culturally significant, concealed or unmasked. *Walter Seidl*

Public Opening: 19. October 2006

www.artreflect.org

Issues of the self and its gradual replacement through various objects, props and prostheses as well as moments of disappearing or publicly shining bodies have permeated photographic art since the 1980s and culminated in the work of Cindy Sherman. With the theoretic support of theorists like Judith Butler or Slavoj Žižek, the physical body has been unmasked as a cultural construct, whose sexual identity is merely one component of the overall functioning of the subject within society.

read more

www.irisklein.com
D: catherine herberstein C: catherine herberstein P: catherine herberstein
A: lenny´s studio M: office@lennysstudio.com

Sarah Schotte
Infographiste - Art Visuel

Online Portefolio

✉ Sarah Schotte

www.sarahschotte.be
D: sarah schotte
M: sarah.schotte@yahoo.fr

---

limited language

limited language

news   about   authors   discussion   ~~articles~~   links   contact

----

why limited

A few years ago, in part to advertise his gallery exhibition, artist Patrick Mimran put up billboards in strategic positions in New York City; one read "to express conceptual ideas write a book, dont paint" another stated "art is not always where you think you are going to find it" Although we do not claim to be in total accord with the artist,s critical intentions these slogans and their occupation of commercial spaces echo our aims.

read the rest of this article

From Art to Design and back again... a proposed lecture on theory and practice

Students of the School of Graphic Design at London College of Printing recently gave the theme of "Relay" to their graduation show. "Relay" acts as both a metaphor and an adjective for Graphic Design and its role in visual culture. The modern city is a matrix of information, mediated through sound, text and image. Graphic Design provides the syntax or visual language for relaying this information.

read the rest of this article

Graphic Design History - Unlisted

Discussion about graphic design so often oscillates between two poles: graphic design as an agent of consumerism or as an art object/subject. At any given moment its definition will be passing from one description to the next. At the moment, for many designers, and writers on design, the aspiration is clearly a move towards art as a legitimate mooring for graphic design history. Here, we are looking at how these particular history(s), polemics and representations materialise in (graphic) design discourse and importantly form a ?context? for the work of contemporary graphic designers.

read the rest of this article

Ticking off the list...

Advertising transforms the world into a shopping list…graphic design's role in visual culture is less concise. In its short history it has been certified 'modern', bowdlerized by artists for its pop culture frisson and challenged by the First Things First manifesto (twice!) for being reduced to serving the tills of commerce. So often, talk about graphic design oscillates between these two poles, graphic design as shopping basket or as art object/subject.

read the rest of this article

www.limitedlanguage.org
D: oskar karlin **C:** oskar karlin **P:** colin davies, monika parrinder
A: limited language.org **M:** info@limitedlanguage.org

{ amazing tree house }

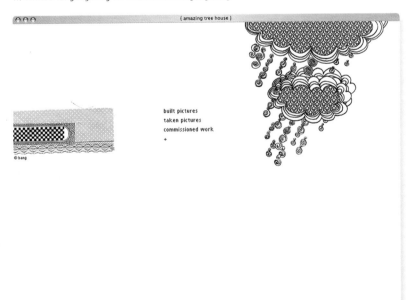

built pictures
taken pictures
commissioned work
+

© bang

www.amazingtreehouse.net
D: jurate gacionyte, bang
A: amazing tree house **M:** bang@amazingtreehouse.net

www.blumencompany.de
D: sandra leister, alexander schäfer C: alexander schäfer
A: 372dpi - design print internet M: a.schaefer@372dpi.com

www.milk-studio.net
D: miriam casanellas C: rubén báez P: rubén báez
A: milk-studio.net M: info@milk-studio.net

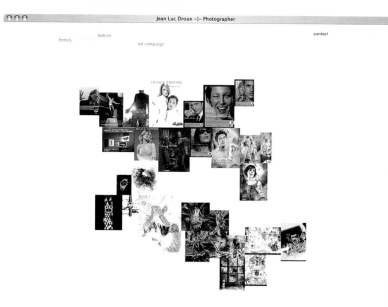

www.jeanlucdroux.com
D: duriez jérémie C: duriez jérémie P: disorder act.
A: disorder M: contact@visiondenuit.com

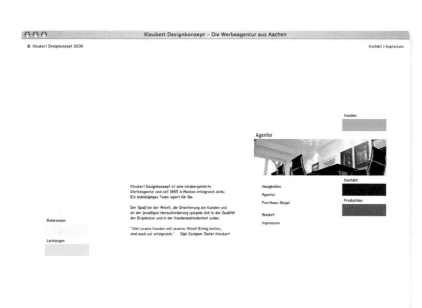

www.kloubert.de
D: domeniceau | bdes. dominik welters P: kloubert designkonzept
A: domeniceau | bdes. dominik welters M: www.domeniceau.de

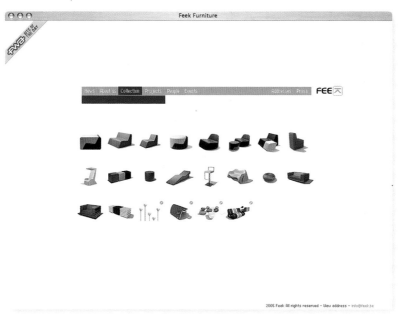

www.feek.be
D: hans mortelmans, nicolas desle C: hans mortelmans, nicolas desle P: syntetik
A: syntetik M: hans@syntetik.be, nicolas@syntetik.be

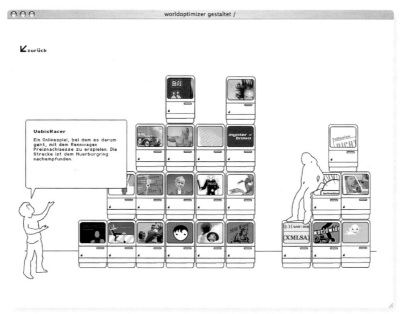

www.worldoptimizer.com
D: b. zwarg, e. wendland, j. ion s., r. hampicke, b. kaulfuß C: l. kwiatkoswki, m. ziebell
A: worldoptimizer M: mail@worldoptimizer.com

www.hellalouie.com
D: bryan louie C: william veasey P: bryan louie
A: hellalouie M: bryankailouie@gmail.com

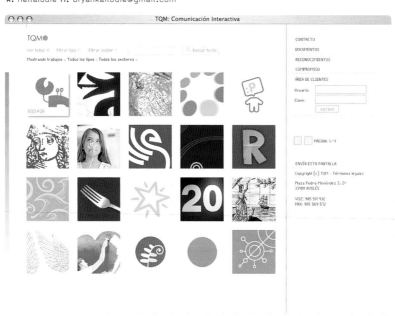

www.trisquel.com
D: tqm team C: tqm team P: tqm team
A: trisquelmedia (tqm) M: estudio@trisquel.com

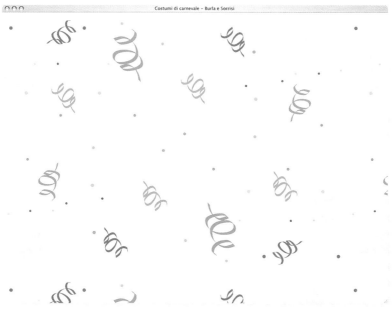

www.burlaesorrisi.it
D: andrea emma C: alfredo esposito P: nicola verazzo
A: www.studiokoine.it M: info@studiokoine.it

○○○ Trafik – Conception graphique + développement multimédia

COLLEKTO
4 PROJETS DE CRÉATIONS COLLECTIVES
PAR TRAFIK. ÉDITIONS PYRAMYD

TRAFIK	DIRECTION ARTISTIQUE + CRÉATION GRAPHIQUE + MULTIMÉDIA	3, PLACE SAINT-VINCENT 69001 LYON TÉL : 04 78 29 16 19 FAX : 04 78 27 63 60	CONTACT NEWSLETTER	SHIFT TYPOTEK
		DOSSIER DE PRESSE	BOUTIQUE	PARTICIPEZ GOODIES

| ÉVÉNEMENTS | MARITHE + FRANÇOIS GIRBAUD
WHO'S NEXT
BOFFI + TRAFIK
SONIK WALL
LE PASS
LOUIS VUITTON | AGNÈS B. / B.DULE
PREMIÈRE VISION
SUPERLUXE
SKETCH
DESIGNER'S DAYS 04 - HABITAT | ICÔNES / ARTAZART
ÉCOLE SUPÉRIEURE D'ART - AIX
H2PTM03
MONBEAUPAYS
SIGNOTEK |

| TRAVAUX | ROSSIGNOL
YES ARCHITECTES
LVM
CHAMONIX
ECOLE D'ARCHITECTURE DE LYON
MUSIQUE EN SCENE
GRAME
DOMESTIC
BODY PACK
DESIGNED BY ®
PACIFIC MOTION
SPORT COMMUNICATION
OXBOW | JAILLANCE
ARCHINOVA
CRAC
POUM - HABITAT
APRIL 77
CENTRE DU DESIGN RHÔNE-ALPES
TECHNIKART
LE VOXX
LE PAVE DANS LA MARE
TRAX
ZONE INTÉRIEURE
PETITS ÉCRITS RÉTICULAIRES | LE CUBE / ART 3000
GALERIE ROGER TATOR
ERASME
WAD
AGFA MONOTYPE LTD
C & C
ROBIN HOOD
SALOMON
KAHLA
CAMPS
ENSSIB
NESSO |

www.lavitrinedetrafik.com
D: trafik
M: trafik.lyon@wanadoo.fr

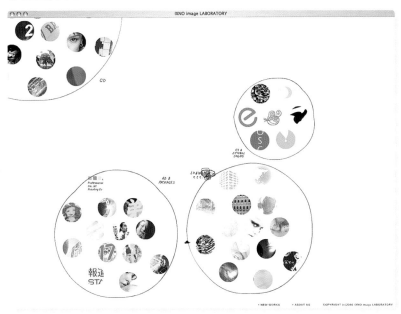

○○○ IXNO image LABORATORY

www.ixno.com
D: ixno image laboratory C: junichi kato (cmd9) P: ixno image laboratory
A: ixno image laboratory M: info@ixno.com

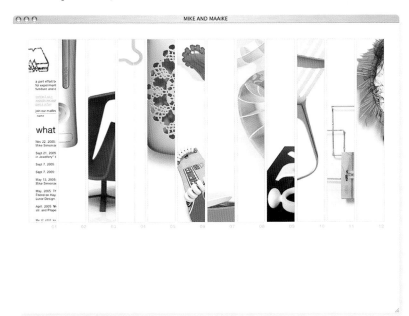

○○○ MIKE AND MAAIKE

www.mikeandmaaike.com
D: maaike evers, mike simonian
A: mike and maaike inc. M: info@mikeandmaaike.com

Devil`s Food Cake

Preheat the oven 180°C
(Gas 4). Grease a deep 20 cm round cake tin
and line the base with baking paper. Sift the
flour, cocoa and bicarbnate of soda into a
large bowl.

Add the sugar to the
sifed dry ingrdients. Combine the buttermilk,
eggs and butter, then pour onto the dry

www.pavlikmicek.com/sweetfood
D: pavel micek
M: www.pavlikmicek.com

dei.ne agentur
für multimedia

deine agentur   **aktuelles**   referenzen   kontakt   netzwerk   impressum
analyse   leistungen   team   agb

analyse. Wir definieren Stärken und Schwächen deines Unternehmens.
konzept. Wir erarbeiten professionelle Lösungen, die die Stärken deines Unternehmens hervorheben und
die Schwachen beseitigen.
entwurf. Das Konzept wird in mehreren Vorschlägen veranschaulicht.
umsetzung. Der ausgewählte Vorschlag wird von uns verwirklicht und in die passenden Medien umgesetzt.
produktion. Wenn erwünscht, kümmern wir uns auch um die Druckerei, Installation, Upload und holen Angebote ein.
projektmanagement. Um keine bösen Überraschungen im Projektablauf zu erleben, begleiten wir dieses vom ersten Kontakt
bis zum fertigen Produkt.

www.deineagentur.at
D: petra wagner, mark poreda C: mark poreda P: petra wagner, mark poreda
A: deine agentur M: poreda@deineagentur.at

ABOUT   OFFERING   PROJECTS   NEWS   CONTACT
Past Projects   Current Projects

gialighting

Projects

G3A

G3A's offices are at lower
ground and basement level,
with very limited natural
light entering the space.
The design challenge was to
make the space feel very
comfortable and naturally lit,
despite the low daylight
levels. This was achieved by
implementing an artificial
daylighting system, linked to
light sensors, which shifts
colour temperature and
intensity during the day,
mimicking the changes that
you experience with natural
light. In addition, various
Decorative lighting effects
were installed, to further
enhance the feeling of
movement and colour. The
lighting scheme transformed
the space from a very dark
and dingy basement,
previously thought only
useful for storage, to high
class office accommodation,
winning the 2006 BCO Award
for best fit out.
more images >

Bonhill

Architecturally the dominant
feature of this space is the
glass wall separating the
exterior courtyard from the
interior. The lighting
scheme was designed to
enhance and visually link the
exterior and interior
elements.

This was achieved by
enhancing the linear shape
of the architecture both
internally and externally with
light. Internally subtle linear
white light accents break the
ceiling line. While more
vibrant blue linear lighting
accents low level details
along the water feature and
curved wall.
more images >

Abraham Lincoln School

This project provided a
number of interesting and
potentially conflicting design
requirements. During the
day, this period building is
used as a school, and in the
evenings for seminars. The
local authorities required
very specific lighting levels
to be met to cater for the
buildings use as a school,
whilst the project client was
keen to preserve and
improve the buildings
historic period appearance.
The structure of the building
was also challenging, with
much of the ceiling and wall
rendering being original
horsehair plaster, without
the recess depth available in
a more modern building.
Careful selection of fittings
and their positioning was
critical to achieving a
successful scheme.
more images >

www.gialighting.co.uk
D: antonin ferla P: gia lighting
A: alex treadway ltd M: info@antoninferla.com, creative@alextreadway.co.uk

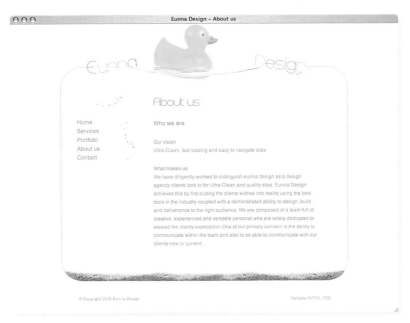

www.eunna.com
D: innocent muranda **C:** benjamin matewe
A: eunna design **M:** info@eunna.com

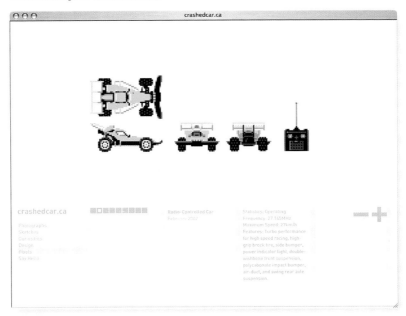

crashedcar.ca
D: paul mcdougall
M: crashedcar@gmail.com

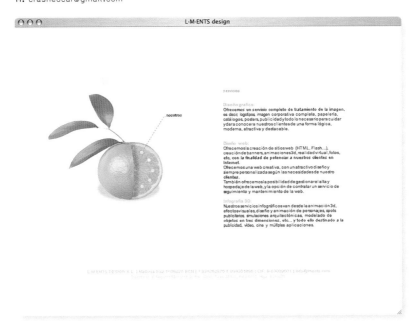

www.lments.com
D: ferran amor
A: l·m·ents design **M:** info@lments.com

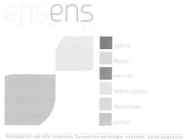

www.ensens.com
D: jc gilquin P: jc gilquin
A: ensens

who am i?

who | what | where

• graphic • multimedia • illustration • photography •
artN2design © 2005 All right reserved

www.artn2design.com
D: nelson pinontoan C: nelson pinontoan P: nelson pinontoan
A: artn2design M: n2@artn2design.com

orangeflux design

rs owens > art award catalog

about us   products   contact us   news   ●

orangeflux portfolio   print   digital   identity   other

To view a piece, simply select from the glowing, orange buttons above. Click on any of them to see a print sample. To view digital (internet, presentations and cd-rom's) samples click the "digital" text button above. "Identity" displays logo and identity work. View miscellaneous projects, such as promotionals, under "other". For our visual recordings, shirts and more, see the "products" section.

www.orangeflux.com
D: kris meyer, matt fey C: kris meyer
A: orangeflux M: mail@orangeflux.com

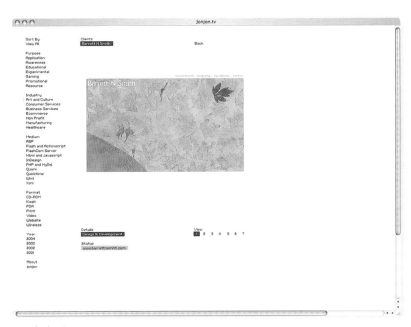

www.jonjon.tv
D: jon montenegro C: jon montenegro P: jon montenegro
A: variousways M: jonm@variousways.com

www.tenbyten.org
D: jonathan harris
A: number 27 M: jjh@number27.org

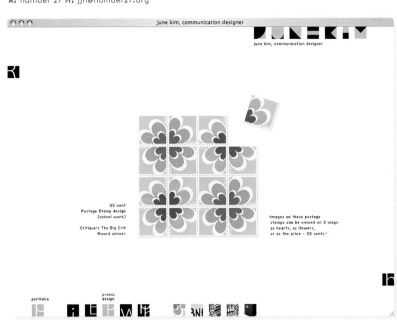

junekim.com
D: june kim C: june kim
M: june@junekim.com

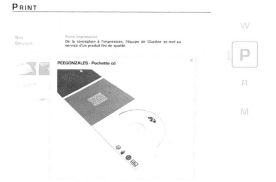

www.glucone.com
D: hollebecq sophie C: videira patrick P: neroucheff micha
A: glucône M: info@glucone.com

www.kunstdichte.com
D: j.antholz C: j.antholz P: klaus bartmann
A: modomoove M: ja@modomoove.de

zelazela.com
D: dushan milic, zela lobb
A: no such animal M: zela@zelazela.com

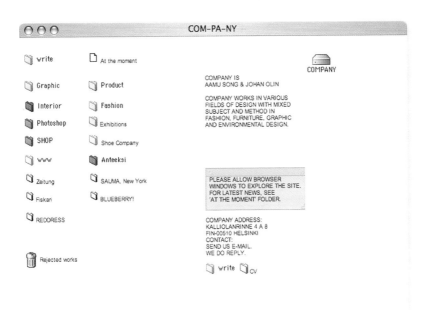

www.com-pa-ny.com
D: johan olin C: johan olin P: company
A: company M: info@com-pa-ny.com

www.davidjosue.com
D: jenaro diaz C: jenaro diaz P: jenaro diaz
A: djnr.net M: djnr@djnr.net

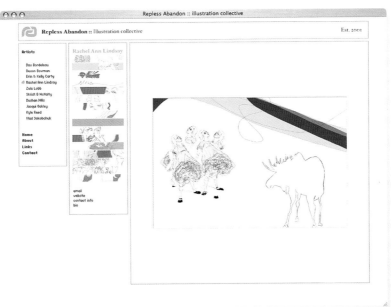

www.replessabandon.com
D: marco cibola, sködt d mcnalty C: marco cibola, sködt d mcnalty
A: nove studio, strange//attraktoR: M: info@novestudio.com, studio@strangeattraktor.com

PATRICK DAVISON · INFO · NEWS   MAIN / LIMITED EDITIONS / PEOPLE AND ANIMALS 13/22

www.patdavisonphotography.com
D: jayson singe C: raymond simmons P: jayson singe
A: neon sky creative media, inc. M: singe@neonsky.com

C.DRIC.BE/GIUM

INDEX
HTTP://C.DRIC.BE/GIUM

WHAT   A crossing between a blog and a collage book.
Rebooted every other week now and then.

02 WALK IN THE RAIN
Uploaded on August 16, 2006

01 MACHINES WITH AN ATTITUDE
Uploaded on August 07, 2006

00 STRANGER THAN WE CAN IMAGINE
Uploaded on July 10, 2006

MADE WITH THE GIMP, XHTML & CSS BY CÉDRIC DE WULF
RSS FEED // REDISCOVER THE WEB. GET FIREFOX

c.dric.be
D: cédric de wulf C: cédric de wulf
M: mail@c.dric.be

Love Bird

NEWS & UPDATES

LOVEBIRD WINS BEST IN SHOW

www.lovebirdagency.com
D: max mancuso, greg washington P: max mancuso, lovebird agency
A: lovebird agency M: info@lovebirdagency.com

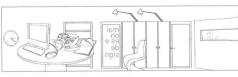

www.maionesedesign.net
D: filipa santos C: helder almeida P: fernado faleiro
A: maionese design M: www@maionesedesign.net

www.airbagindustries.com
D: greg storey
A: airbag industries, llc M: greg@gregstorey.com

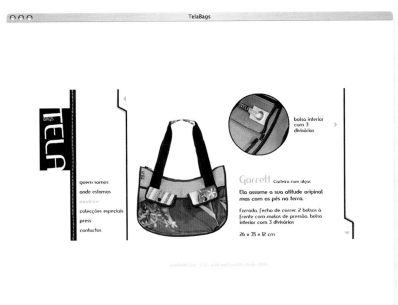

www.telabags.net
D: simão c. almeida C: simão c. almeida P: simão c. almeida
A: slide - web and graphic studio M: info@slidestudio.com.pt

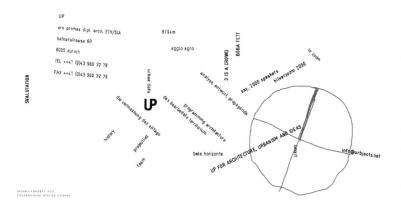

www.urbjects.net
D: k72, franziska eriksen C: cornel rüegg P: k72
A: k72 M: www.k72.ch

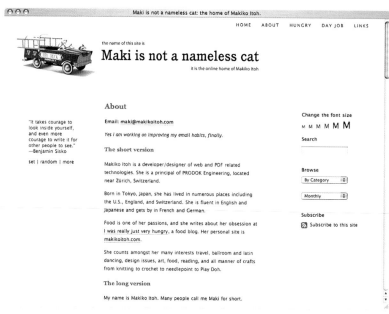

www.makikoitoh.com
D: makiko itoh
M: maki@makikoitoh.com

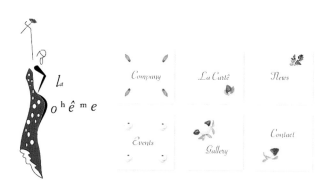

www.bohemejavea.com
D: anna lópez, paco costa C: david pons P: delaweb, s.l.
A: delaweb, s.l.

www.mephistoproject.com
D: ilaria boz C: maurizio albertoni P: dps srl
A: dps srl M: info@dpsonline.it

www.wendykwei.com
D: wendy kwei, wacker eins P: wendy kwei
M: info@wendykwei.com

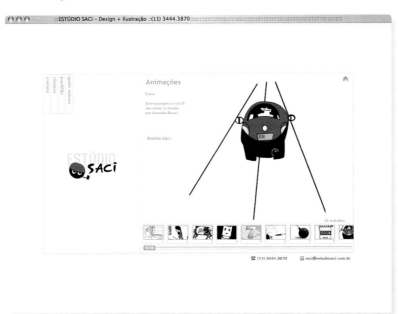

www.estudiosaci.com.br
D: zé mario passos, carvall C: zé mario passos P: estúdio saci
A: estúdio saci M: saci@estudiosaci.com.br

www.miresweb.com
D: david pinedo, maribel paez **C:** miquel lópez
A: mires edc **M:** mires@miresweb.com

webundso.ch
D: noël girstmair **C:** noël girstmair **P:** noël girstmair
A: webundso gmbh **M:** noel@webundso.ch

www.nexussr.com
D: tqm team **C:** tqm team **P:** maderas seivane
A: trisquelmedia (tqm) for maderas seivane **M:** estudio@trisquel.com

www.meetingyou.es
D: jorge edwards gutiérrez, joseba ares bermejo C: j. a. bermejo P: ecequiel barricart
A: you media M: joseba@youmedia.es

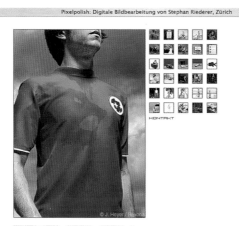

www.pixelpolish.ch
D: marc rinderknecht C: marc rinderknecht P: marc rinderknecht
A: kobebeef M: mr@kobebeef.ch

www.jamesjean.com
D: james jean
A: process recess M: mail@jamesjean.com

qian qian

NEWS
DESIGN
ILLUSTRATION
MOTION
INFO
MISC

The Current Group
Trends
Sketchel
Get It Louder
Hang On The Box
Credo Poster
Yawn
MSU Brochure
Q2design
Bloody Mickey
Zone Architects
Moto V750
Think UK

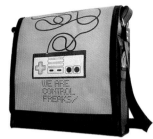

q2design.com
D: qian qian
M: info@q2design.com

__Portfolio digital

++ +
++ **PORTFOLIO**

ILUSTRAÇÃO
IC / BRANDING
PRINT
WEB / DIGITAL

++ **PROJECTOS**

www.esquissos.com
D: plinio goncalves gomes
A: esquissos M: p.gomes@esquissos.com

www.antoninferla.com
D: antonin ferla C: julien ferla
A: antonin ferla M: info@antoninferla.com

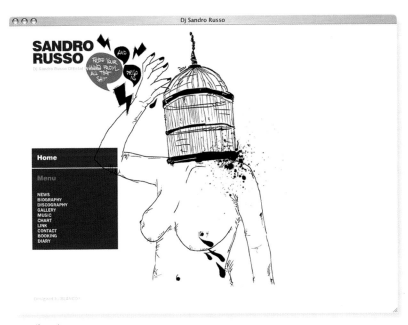

www.djsandrorusso.com
D: studioblanco, krghettojuice.com C: studioblanco, krghettojuice.com P: studioblanco
A: studioblanco M: krghettojuice@hotmail.com

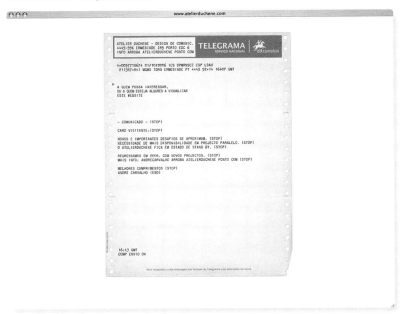

www.atelierduchene.com
D: andré carvalho C: andré carvalho P: andré carvalho
A: atelierduchene M: info@atelierduchene.com

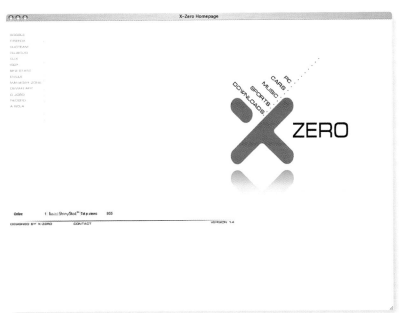

x-zero.planetaclix.pt
D: x-zero
M: x-zero@clix.pt

timo koskinen
portfolio
contact

timo**koskinen**

student of architecture ■

helsinki university of technology
department of architecture

74% of studies completed

student of arts ■

university of art and design helsinki
department of interior architecture
and furniture design

for a complete curriculum vitae
please send your contact information
to cv@timokoskinen.com

www.timokoskinen.com
D: timo koskinen C: timo koskinen
M: info@timokoskinen.com

Die Schmuckstücke   Die Köchinnen   Die Herstellung   Der Kontakt

und , die beiden
Perlenköchinnen, haben sich 2001 als Radiofrauen
kennengelernt. Und konnten sich nicht leiden. Kein Wunder: Die
eine blond, die andere dunkel. Die eine gross, die andere klein.
Die eine mit Vorliebe für den Kulturteil in der Zeitung, die
andere für Horoskope. Und dennoch haben sie sich gefunden –
durch ihre Leidenschaft für handgefertigten Schmuck, für Perlen,
die jedes Décolleté zum Blickfang machen, für Experimente mit
PVC, Farben und Formen. Und wenn sie heute stundenlang
zusammen in der Perlenküche sitzen, diskutieren sie halt über
den People-Teil der Zeitung – der interessiert sie nämlich beide.

www.perlenkueche.ch
D: andrea heimgartner C: stefan schnürle P: perlenküche
M: andrea.heimgartner@bluewin.ch

BOOKS CHARACTERS MISC

for UTEL, MART agency

www.grivina.ru
D: oksana grivina
M: oksana@grivina.ru

www.davidmarthan.com
D: david marthan P: david marthan
M: david@davidmarthan.com

www.akvarij.hr
D: jelena bakotin C: jelena bakotin
A: digital studio akvarij M: jelena@akvarij.hr, yelle75@yahoo.com

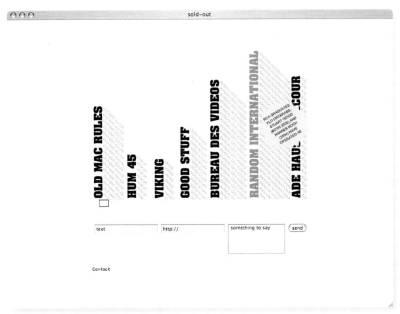

www.sold-out.ch
D: gaël hugo C: gaël hugo P: gaël hugo
A: sold-out.ch M: mail@sold-out.ch

uni.extrasmallstudio.com/gr05
D: letizia bollini C: criticalbit
A: extrasmallstudio M: www.extrasmallstudio.com

www.vhox.com
D: thierry houillon C: michael montmoril P: michael montmoril
A: vhox M: michael@vhox.com

www.puregrafico.com
D: rubén martínez C: rubén martínez P: rubén martínez
A: puré M: info@puregrafico.com

www.dulidu.com/indice.htm
D: duli*du
M: duli@dulidu.com

www.ursulacuesta.de
D: diego gardón P: ursula cuesta
M: ursulacuesta@hotmail.com

www.bix.at
D: jan edler C: third place P: jan edler, tim edler
A: realities:united architects M: info@realu.de

www.designideias.com
D: margarida almeida, carlos pinto
A: designideias M: comercial@designideias.com

\ \ \ \ \ LSDspace \

La intención de todo buen packaging es aumentar el valor y volumen de las ventas, probando la eficacia y el éxito de la marca. Pero lo más importante, desde el punto de vista del diseño, es que el packaging es una manifestación sencilla, sucinta y desnuda de la marca. *Turner Duckworth*

packaging

packaging carteles editorial logos identidad tipografía espacios talleres web en los libros info | contacto LSDspace

lustau kortext vendin estilo happy new brand

lustau

sherry solera reserva, propuesta de rediseño | etiquetas y embalajes lustau one y lustau trilogy

www.lsdspace.com
D: gabriel martínez, sonia díaz, cristina hernanz C: c. h. hernández P: lsdspace design
A: la cuchara no existe M: www.lacucharanoexiste.net

:::::MASAGRIS:::::

www.masagris.cl
D: miguel morales, fernando jorquera, nicolas lundin
A: masagris M: contacto@masagris.cl

www.baxterphoto.com
D: todd baxter
M: todd@baxterphoto.com

www.ad-g.it
D: davide g. aquini
M: info@ad-g.it

www.verslevin.com/
D: vlad turcu P: isabelle queyraud
A: ergo sum M: iqueyraud@ergosum.fr

WHAT'S COOKIN'

Designing with passion
SATURDAY, OCTOBER 28, 2006 @ 21:54

One obvious and another less obvious steal or rip-off (as you wish to call it) came to my eyes recently. In article 1 is this a rip-off?" I pointed obvious one, and in the comments to the article I pointed one less obvious. Both of them are inspired by my design. What's wrong with those people? Do they know how to design a blog or what? Well, since these two are the first rip-offs of my blog design, I decided to write an article about designing with passion, maybe the guys will learn something ;)

And yes, there is an easy way of designing a "killer website". Here are few tips that help me design.

Continue reading »

RECENTLY IN THE CUISINE

CSS image replacement techniques
SATURDAY, OCTOBER 21, 2006 @ 21:33

When you are engaged in web design process, one of the most helpful things is CSS image replacement technique. In this article, I will show you the basics you should know for replacing text with images. I will show you how to use a logo for Heading 1 (which is widely used for displaying company logo), how to replace different headings, and the last but not least - how to use this technique to display engaging and beautiful navigation.

Continue reading »

Create your own drop down menu with nested submenus using CSS and a little JavaScript
WEDNESDAY, OCTOBER 11, 2006 @ 22:57

Drop down menus are among the coolest things on the web. Beside that they are also very good for creating navigations that contain many elements. The main problems of creating drop down menus lies in the Internet Explorer's inappropriate way of displaying :hover pseudo class (not recognized anywhere except in A tag), and the problem in calculating the z-index when an element is positioned absolutely inside a relatively positioned element.

www.emanuelblagonic.com
D: emanuel blagonic
A: omnicron **M:** emanuel@emanuelblagonic.com

www.emphasis.ro
D: emil manolea **P:** emphasis studio
A: emphasis studio **M:** office@emphasis.ro

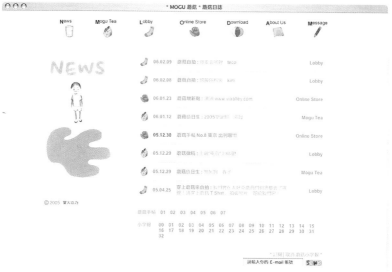

www.mogu.com.tw
D: mei-yu lee **P:** johnny chang
A: booday workshop limited **M:** johnny@mogu.com.tw

www.brigitte-zarm.de
D: peter luttke C: frank jansen P: frank jansen
A: kunstraummedien M: www.kunstraummedien.de

www.gr0w.com
D: jonathan tan C: paul whitrow
A: grow collective M: www.gr0w.com

www.freshbranding.co.uk
D: joshua hughes
A: fresh branding M: mail@freshbranding.co.uk

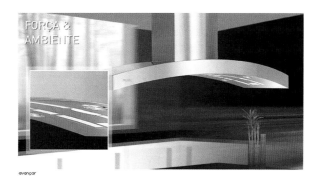

www.frasa.pt
D: joão ramos C: thiago brito P: sérgio ferreira
A: redicom M: www.redicom.pt

www.green-selection.de
D: diego gardón, petra neukirchen
M: www.diegogardon.de

www.reachgroupconsulting.com
D: paul jarvis, ben hulse C: paul jarvis
A: twothirty M: www.twothirty.com

praegnanz.de/weblog

Livesuche >

weblog   essays   portfolio   archiv   info

Prägnanz & Pragmatik	▼
Abonnieren	▼
Kürzlich kommentiert	▼
Andere Weblogs	▼
Aktuelle Linktipps	▼
Gerrit knipst	▼

Okt 2006
27 | Das nächste Webdesignbloggerbuch :-)

Diesmal hat der geschätzte Vladimir Simovic zugeschlagen und zusammen mit Jan Heinicke einen dicken Wälzer über Webdesign mit CSS verfasst.

Das ganze ist außergewöhnlich dick und umfangreich und flößt auf den ersten Blick eine Menge Respekt ein. Ich habe dankenswerterweise ein Rezensionsexemplar vom Verlag erhalten und werde mich nun hüten, nicht darüber zu bloggen. Allerdings muss ich eine fundierte Meinung über das Werk erst einmal zurückstellen, denn ich hatte bisher noch keine Zeit, mir das in aller Ruhe anzugucken. Was ich bisher gesehen habe, war aber sehr gut, ausführlich und sachlich korrekt beschrieben - allein eine gewisse Würze im Schreibstil vermisste ich.

Aber ich bin ja auch generell kein Buch-Typ. Weiß aber gleichzeitig, dass nicht alle angehenden Webdesigner Bock haben, sich die ganzen CSS-Techniken häppchenweise aus dem Netz zu ziehen, wie wir das alle in der Zeit von 2003 bis 2005 gemacht haben. Insofern ist es schon gut, dass es jetzt Bücher gibt, die alle diese Techniken beschreiben und hübsch zusammenfassen. Und dieses dürfte wohl das bisher umfassendste sein.

www.praegnanz.de
D: gerrit van aaken
M: gerrit@praegnanz.de

www.frimidia.it
D: giorgio facoetti C: giorgio facoetti P: giorgio facoetti
A: frimidia M: www.frimidia.it

www.farahzadart.com
D: elena gargiulo P: giorgio gramegna
A: mac@work consulting s.r.l. M: giorgio@macatwork.net

CURRENT ISSUE | GET INVOLVED | PURCHASE | **ADVERTISE** | ABOUT NEED

We are not out
to save the
world, but to
tell the stories
of, and assist,
those who are.

Premiere Issue Winter 2006 Contents

Departments:
ONE | HOME | KIDS | WORK | **HEALTH** |
GENEROSITY | FUTURE | COOPERATION |
DIALOGUE

Featured Organizations | **Current Contributors**

| COOPERATION |

writer: HANNAH RIESGRAF
photographer: LESLIE SPURLOCK
interviewer: KYRA CARPENTER

A volunteer from Littleton, Colorado works with the owner to
level the structure of his home.

A team on assignment with NEED magazine over
a two-week period in July 2006, witnessed
firsthand the hurdles that Gulf Coast residents
and volunteers from across the country have to
face every day. The team saw neighborhoods
that remain disaster zones resembling Third
World countries in the US.

Boards are hauled out of a house in the upper 9th ward by a
Common Ground volunteer.

www.needmagazine.com
D: kelly kinnunen C: kelly kinnunen P: kelly kinnunen
A: need communications M: info@needmagazine.com

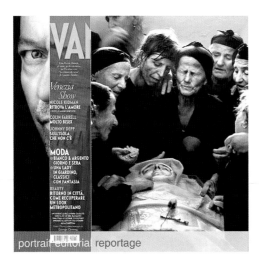

maki galimberti

User :
Password :

»Login

www.makigalimberti.com
D: andrea dall´ara C: alessandro affronto P: giorgio gramegna
A: mac@work consulting s.r.l. M: giorgio@macatwork.net

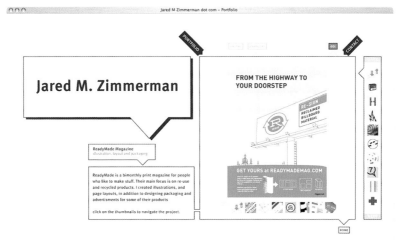

jaredzimmerman.com
D: jared zimmerman
A: fairhouse M: zimmergram@jaredzimmerman.com

juliaabelmann.com
D: julia abelmann C: evan ehat
A: julia abelmann photography M: julia@juliaabelmann.com

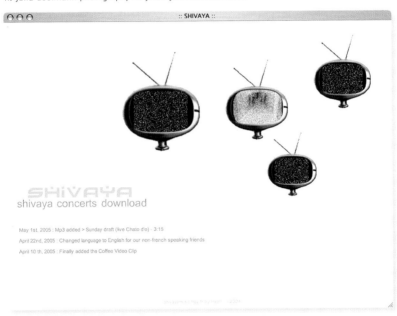

shivaya concerts download

May 1st, 2005 : Mp3 added > Sunday draft (live Chato d'o) - 3:15

April 22nd, 2005 : Changed language to English for our non-french speaking friends

April 10 th, 2005 : Finally added the Coffee Video Clip

shivayamusic.free.fr
D: fred pinault
M: brucelee@worldemail.com

blog   about   photos   archives

The Disc Jockey: Alternate Theories

November 6, 2006: 7:33 PM

(Blog Soundtrack: Louis Armstrong - A Kiss to Build a Dream On. Open it in a new tab/window and read along)

I have, in the past, had a tendency to describe the purpose of my job in terms of entertaining people. Now entering my fifth year of spinning music for parties and weddings on the weekend, it occurs to me that perhaps this little job of mine is quite a lot more meaningful, and for deeper reasons, than I had originally figured.

The purpose of the DJ is to stimulate population growth.

Not a lot of things facilitate sexual relations quite like a night on the town, or close quarters at a party with drinks and music playing. Dancing, to be sure, is a very special brand of public affection that often enough leads to the private sort afterwards.

That said, consider for a moment a few (blatantly unverified but hypothetically accurate) estimates.

Currently Enjoying

Video: Let's Paint, Excercise, and Blend Drinks! is about as crazy as anything you'll watch today.

Video: Grand Theft Mario.

How to Read People.

Ever hear about The Dark Side of the Rainbow? Well, now someone's gone and compiled the audio and video together in sync. Pretty trippy!

Bill Murray attends student party, does dishes

Scarlett Johansson to record an album of Tom Waits covers? This... is awesome.

Video: Idol is like a children's fable, on a copious amount of LSD.

Video: Timelapse leaves me awestruck, music and all.

What would the world be if humans simply stopped existing, right now?

philrenaud.com
D: phil renaud
M: phil@riotindustries.com

DANCE IN BANGKOK

Contemporary , Ballet, Modern
and Modern-Jazz dance classes with
Yoona Crals and **Patrice Leroy**
freelance dance teachers in Bangkok/Thailand.

History and information about Ballet
and Contemporary dance.

contemporary dance
ballet
modern jazz
schedule
schools
volunteering
portfolio
resume
links
contact

News
August | September 2006

**Contemporary Dance Class
at Alliance Francaise**
Thursday
7-9pm / Adult Beginner
New Session will start beginning of October
Prior subscription is required in September

**Modern Jazz dance
at Alliance Francaise**

www.danceinbangkok.com
D: patrice leroy
A: dynamic-e-motion M: patrice@dynamic-e-motion.com

Illustration

Hier finden Sie eine Auswahl einiger Illustrationen, welche ich für Kunden direkt, über eine Agentur
oder privat gezeichnet habe.

· Illustration

www.spadesdesign.de
D: andré hanreich C: andré hanreich P: andre hanreich
A: spades design & illustration M: www.spadesdesign.de

www.thewebflight.com
D: warangkana kanjanachusak, narongyod mahittivanicha C: narongyod m. P: warangkana k.
A: thewebflight co.,ltd. M: info@thewebflight.com

enjoy the clouds

Reneé Rupcich
chitchat@reneerupcich.com

www.reneerupcich.com
D: reneé rupcich
M: chitchat@reneerupcich.com

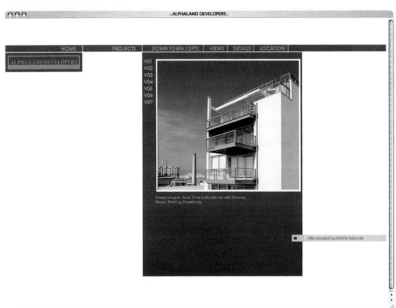

www.lofts.gr
D: stathis kaloudis
M: skaloudis@yahoo.com

www.semerano.com
D: massimo romano **C:** samuel gentile
A: liquid diamond **M:** www.liquiddiamond.it

www.zerkdi-fils.com
D: marie-céline hervé
A: www.unpoissondanslatasse.fr M: marie.herve@unpoissondanslatasse.fr

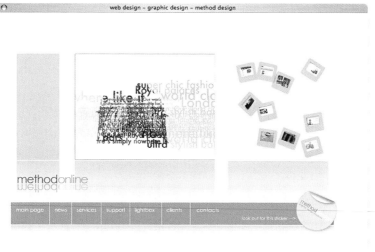

www.method.org.uk
D: james roberts
A: method M: info@method.org.uk

www.tvd-online.de
D: sandra leister, alexander schäfer C: alexander schäfer, kai pahl
A: 372dpi - design print internet M: a.schaefer@372dpi.com

www.underscan.de
D: ellen roth (rosaroth) C: philemon schmidt P: markward wagner
A: rosaroth M: mail@rosaroth.net

www.bob-magazine.com
D: alois gstöttner C: s. hanig, scalar P: alois gstöttner
A: blois.at - büro für visuelle kommunikation M: alois.gstoettner@club-bellevue.com

www.andreaswannerstedt.se
D: andreas wannerstedt C: andreas wannerstedt P: andreas wannerstedt
A: foedus M: andreas@wannerstedt.se

La Fuente de la música

Web realizada en motivo de la presentación de este proyecto realizado por Roland Olbeter y Miguel Rubio.

© ALBERT CLARET / graphic & web design . T 93 317 77 80 . Petritxol 12, 08002 Barcelona . info@albertclaret.com .

www.albertclaret.com
D: albert claret
M: info@albertclaret.com

www.sophiedvorak.com
D: sophie dvorák C: sebastian hanig
A: scalar M: box@scalar.at

www.phapak.net
D: peter hapak C: zoltan szalay P: zoltan szalay
A: dred M: phapak@phapak.net

www.changeisgood.fr
D: júlia vieira C: júlia vieira P: change is good
A: change is good M: www.changeisgood.fr

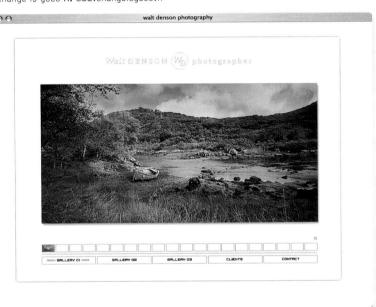

www.waltdenson.com
D: marci peters P: marci peters
A: walt denson photographer M: walt@waltdenson.com

www.gythamander.com
D: casey berman, michael moskowitz C: gabriel hernandez
M: cbb@gythamander.com

Tommaso Mei
Photographer

TEMPORARY SITE

music courtesy of jetlag

Via Filippine degli Organi 8
20135 Milano

+39 335 14 02 466
tommaso.mei@gmail.com

www.tommasomei.it
D: davide bernardi
M: tommaso.mei@gmail.com

STUDIO WAUTERS

www.studiowauters.com
D: hollebecq sophie C: videira patrick P: neroucheff micha
A: glucône M: info@glucone.com

philrouge

www.philrouge.be
D: philippe vermeiren C: philippe vermeiren
A: philrouge photography M: info@philrouge.be

avenuenewyork.com
D: john white
A: avenue M: john@avenuenewyork.com

www.randeepbhoker.com
D: agosh rao C: neeks

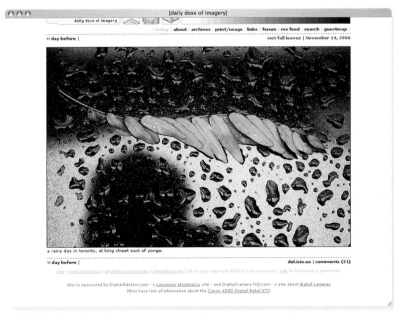

wvs.topleftpixel.com
D: sam javanrouh C: sam javanrouh
M: sam@topleftpixel.com

michael dürr photography
new | portraits | magazines | advertising | movies | contact

design © reya-d : photography © michael durr | all rights reserved

www.michaelduerr.com
D: rafal kosakowski C: rafal kosakowski
A: reya-d M: mike.d@aon.at

marcelweisheit.com

Marcel Weisheit
Random work overview

By update
By name
information/contact
| Search

1 2 3

Repackaging
Tuesday
Jeder siebte Mensch
Kurz davor ist es passiert
Action concept/various
Pimping
Frenzbikushcha/various
Eilers Werke
Photography/various
C-action.com
Stroer
Mars
Photography/people/men
Where is Waldo for idiots
Free Hardcore Porn
Outdoors
fine/fix3D/video mode/various
Photography/people/women
Photography/people/kids
Photography/people/babies
Kampfansage DVD menu
Presents in disguise
Issble
Words are like charms
Kampfansage/various
Slamartist.com/photography
The Clown
Brunnen.de
K Stunts
Kampfansage/print

1 2 3 4 5 6 7 8 9 10 11 12 13 14
Anna, analog, 1995

marcelweisheit.com
D: marcel weisheit C: tobiashartmann.com
A: marcelweisheit.com M: marcel@marcelweisheit.com

http://www.pavlikmicek.com/silvi/

www.pavlikmicek.com/silvi
D: pavlik micek C: pavlik micek P: pavlik micek
A: pavlikmicek M: studio@pavlikmicek.com

SPRINGFIELD--Cortefiel. Puig

www.rlazaro.com
D: estudio rosa lazaro C: jacinto lana P: estudio rosa lazaro
A: estudio rosa lazaro M: jacinto@masmac.com

www.vectorsesh.com
D: ben hewitt C: ben hewitt P: ben hewitt
A: vectorsesh M: ben@vectorsesh.com

www.carlosportugal.pt
D: adriano esteves C: alexandre gomes, ricardo simão P: bürocratik
A: bürocratik M: info@burocratik.com

www.sisterface.com
D: enrique pastor de luz C: enrique pastor de luz
A: sisterface M: enrique.pastor@sisterface.com

www.artworksgroup.net
D: yongil lee C: bonghee kim P: yongil lee
A: artworksgroup M: webmaster@artworksgroup.net

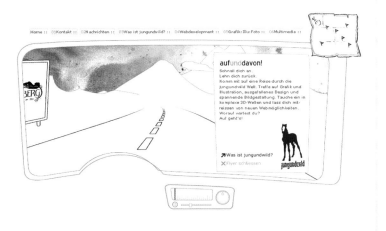

www.jungundwild.com
D: leo glomann C: leo glomann P: leo glomann
A: jungundwild M: leo.glomann@jungundwild.com

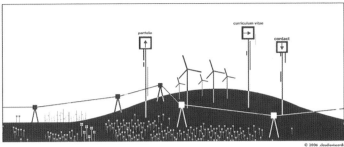

www.claudioviscardi.it
D: claudio viscardi
M: mail@claudioviscardi.it

ki2n.com
D: king yip P: king yip
A: the k!2n. M: king@ki2n.com

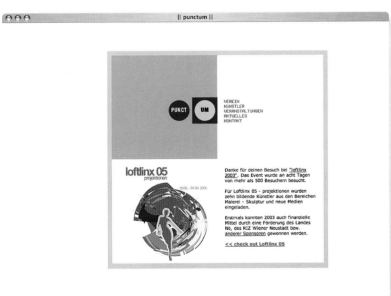

www.kulturpunctum.at
D: dietmar halbauer C: dietmar halbauer P: embers consulting gmbh
A: embers consulting gmbh M: d.halbauer@embers.at

heidi langauer

home | aktuell | biografie | werke | bibliografie | links

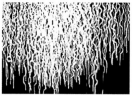 

§ | design: mann & maus

e-mail: info@heidilangauer.ch | telefon: ++41 (0)44 481 91 81

www.heidilangauer.ch/
D: rolf eberle **C:** rolf eberle **P:** rolf eberle
A: mann & maus **M:** eberle@mannundmaus.ch

Memoria Histórica de la Alameda

la memoria   cultural luggage   grupo de trabajo   enlaces   contactos

"Es mejor quedarse callado y olvidar. Es lo único que debemos hacer. Tenemos que olvidar. Y esto no va a ocurrir abriendo casos, mandando a la gente a la cárcel. OL-VI-DAR: esta es la palabra, y para que esto ocurra, los dos lados tienen que olvidar y seguir trabajando."

(Ex general Augusto Pinochet, 13 de septiembre de 1995, dos días después del 22º aniversario del golpe militar)

"Los distintos modos de represión, tanto como la propaganda individualista elitaria y el negocio, constituyen las modalidades culturales propias de un proyecto que para rediseñar un país a la medida de lo que el proyecto espera y por ende, para perdurar, requiere de la **confiscación de la memoria**, del temor consecuente y de la apropiación de los espacios intelectivos del pueblo, la jerarquización y la uniformación totalitaria de la vida."

("Para no morir de hambre en el arte", Fundamentacion, Colectivo de Accion De Arte · 1979)

⊞ PERSPECTÍVA PARCIAL SOBRE LA MEMORIA

Cada palabra que se detenga demasiado tiempo en el mismo lugar de sentido pierde su fuerza, su posibilidad de acción. Queremos otorgar a memoria otros y múltiples sentidos al fin de producir una constelación de perspectivas parciales y simultáneas, capaces más de crear un ámbito de diálogo que un enunciado definitorio.

"Es una forma de recuperación y activación de experiencias y acontecimientos de lo vivido, en la ciudad y en sus habitantes".
"Forma de trueque donde manda la economía del recuerdo y del olvido".
"Condensador que acumula experiencias de tiempo y de espacio por liberarlas con un nivel de energía superior".
"Juego que demistifica el tiempo cambiando la orientación de días, semanas, años".
"Producto incesante de la ciudad y del vivir social. Escombro".
"Lo que está sempre ocurriendo, que siempre se está creando y almacenando, de manera implícita o esplícita, en el cuerpo, en nuestra materialidad mnemonica".
"Proceso de recuperación doloroso, largo y reversible, opuesto de amputación".

⊞ MAPA Y CONTENIDOS DE LA MEMORIA DE LA ALAMEDA

El mapa que aquí pueden ver es el dibujo GPS-Drawing del recorrido del 1 de julio 2005, día del estreno sobre la Alameda de las Delicias.

www.memorialameda.cl
D: david boardman **C:** david boardman **P:** netzfunk.org
A: netzfunk.org **M:** d-@netzfunk.org

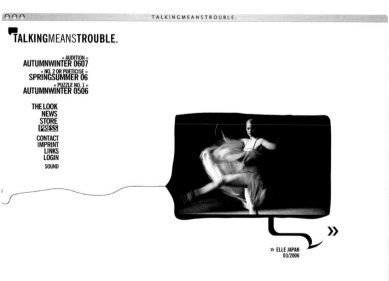

TALKINGMEANS**TROUBLE.**

« AUDITION »
AUTUMNWINTER 0607
« NO. 2 OR POETICISE »
SPRINGSUMMER 06
« PUZZLE NO. 1 »
AUTUMNWINTER 0506

THE LOOK
NEWS
STORE
PRESS
CONTACT
IMPRINT
LINKS
LOGIN
SOUND

» ELLE JAPAN
03/2006

»

#

www.talkingmeanstrouble.com
D: b_utop b:uro d.es_senses
M: mail@b-utop.de

www.playoutdesign.com
D: tiago machado C: tiago machado P: tiago machado
A: playoutdesign M: info@playoutdesign.com

ANTEEKSI DESIGNS <u>HAPPENINGS</u>, <u>PUBLICATIONS</u>, <u>PRODUCTS</u>, <u>CLOTHES</u>, <u>BUILDINGS</u> AND CITIES. **ANTEEKSI** IS 14 <u>PEOPLE</u> IN KALLIO, HELSINKI. CONTACT **ANTEEKSI** : <u>info@anteeksi.org</u>. <u>Anteeksi Uutiset #1</u> <u>Anteeksi Uutiset #2</u> <u>Anteeksi Uutiset #3</u> **ANTEEKSI** <u>EXHIBITIONS</u>, **ANTEEKSI** <u>INTERIORS</u>, **ANTEEKSI** <u>EDUCATION</u>.

ANTEEKSI *METSÄ* /
ANTEEKSI *FOREST* /
in Norsu Gallery, Helsinki.
20th October to 25th November.
Big kiitos to all opening party
people!

SEE INSIDE ANTEEKSI: <u>COM-PA-NY</u>, <u>M41LH2</u>, <u>AO ARCHITECTS</u>, <u>VIRE-DESIGN</u>, <u>NOW OFFICE</u>, <u>LACQUER</u>.

www.anteeksi.org
D: johan olin,anteeksi
A: anteeksi M: info@anteeksi.org

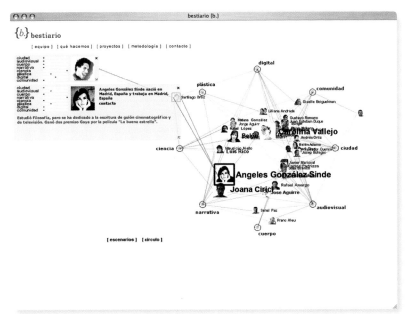

bestiario.org
D: santiago ortiz, andres ortiz C: santiago ortiz P: santiago ortiz, andrés ortiz
A: bestiario M: santiago@bestiario.org

www.artenuevo.be
D: jan van der waerden C: jan van der waerden P: jan van der waerden
A: arte nuevo bvba M: info@artenuevo.be

www.urbanlandscape.org.uk
D: peter marshall C: peter marshall P: peter marshall
A: peter marshall & mike seaborne M: petermarshall@cix.co.uk

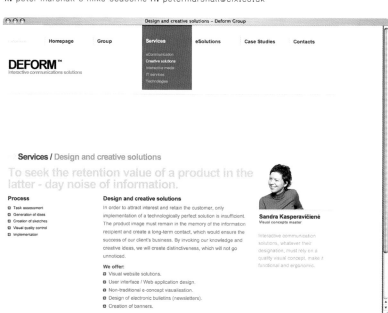

www.deform-group.com
D: andrius kuciauskas C: domas juknevicius, aurimas juncis P: andrius kuciauskas
A: deform-group M: info@deform-group.com

superlover.com.au
D: justin maller
M: justin@superlover.com.au

www.ellhnikodesign.com
D: theo gennitsakis C: paris athens P: visual designer
A: ellhnikodesign M: theogennitsakis@gmail.com

www.marleennoordergraaf.com
D: michiel stoop C: michiel stoop P: marleen noordergraaf
A: beelders M: info@beelders.nl

Work | Contact | Links

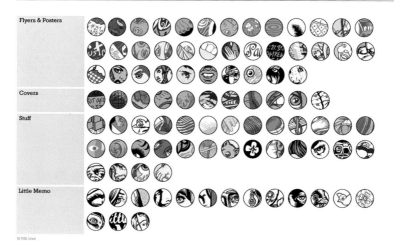

Flyers & Posters

Covers

Stuff

Little Memo

www.zeloot.nl
D: zeloot C: bastiaan de boer P: zeloot
A: zeloot M: info@zeloot.nl

..::: Portfolio Personal ::: Diseños|EBQ :::..

EBQ
PORTFOLIO
CONTACTO
NEWS

www.disenosebq.com
D: esteban bonet quiles
A: diseños|ebq M: info@disenosebq.com

loldibus : lot of love dibus, by fernandezcoca.com. Ilustrador, illustration, illustrazione, ilustração, Abbildung

by fernandezcoca.com

español   english
italiano   deutsch
português françáis
           català

loldibus.com by fernandezcoca.com [loldibus@fernandezcoca.com] +34 971 70 74 22 . España/Spain.

www.loldibus.com
D: antonio fernández-coca C: mediadvanced.com, fernandezcoca.com
M: studio@fernandezcoca.com

www.movinord.com
D: ken C: spi
A: ken M: www.ken.es

news

13. July 2006
Das Tutorial zur gleichzeitigen Installation von php4 und phph5 wurde über 1.000 mal gedowloaded

5. July 2006
plan08 erweitert sein Angebot an kostenlosen Services um ein Tool zum Erstellen von Farbkarten aus Internetseiten.

17. June 2006
Die Hotelgruppe Feriotel beauftragt plan08 mit dem Entwurf und der Umsetzung ihres Internetauftritts.

plan08

Als Agentur für neue Medien liegen unsere Kern-Kompetenzen im Bereich **Webentwicklung, Suchmaschinen Optimierung, Online Marketing, Webdesign** und **Konzeptionierung Ihrer Online Strategien.**
Hauptaugenmerk haben wir dabei auf die Entwicklung von individuellen Online Lösungen gelegt. Es ist uns eine Freude für unsere Kunden Produkte zu entwickeln, die es bisher so nicht auf dem Markt gab. Herausforderungen sind bei plan08 immer herzlich willkommen. Die Kompetenzen unserer Agentur gliedern sich in drei Hauptgruppen: **projekt08** - spezialisiert auf die Entwicklung von Webanwendungen, **studio08** - dem Kreativ-Team und **web08** die Abteilung für Branchenlösungen.

Der Mensch steht bei unserer Arbeit stets im Vordergrund. Deshalb legen wir neben der optimalen technischen Umsetzung viel Wert auf einen engen Kontakt zum Kunden und darauf, dass die von uns entwickelten Webseiten den aktuellen Standards der Usability entsprechen.

plan08 wurde im Jahre 1999 gegründet und ist somit eine der ältesten Softwareschmieden mit Online Schwerpunkt Freiburgs.

Nils Langner

www.plan08.de
D: nils langner C: nils langner P: nils langner
A: plan08 M: www.plan08.de

www.subcutanspoon.com
D: quim tarrida C: subcutanspoon P: subcutanspoon
A: subcutanspoon M: info@subcutanspoon.com

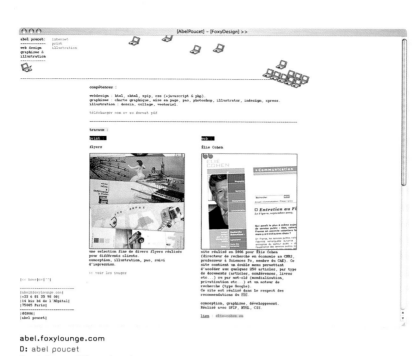

abel.foxylounge.com
D: abel poucet
M: abel.poucet@laposte.net

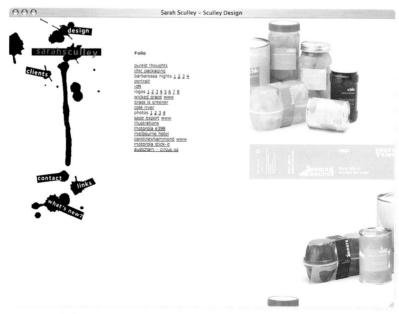

www.disgenia.net
D: alejandro ochoa alonso
M: info@disgenia.net

www.sculleydesign.com
D: sarah sculley
A: sculley design M: sarah@sculleydesign.com

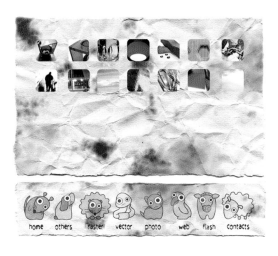

www.animaisa.ru
D: lebedeva tat`yana
M: art@animaisa.ru

www.45royale.com
D: matt downey C: matt downey
A: 45royale, inc. M: info@45royale.com

madreal.com
D: derrick hodgson, kyle mcintosh C: kyle mcintosh
A: popgun media M: popgunmedia.com

blog.deesigns.de
D: stefan schleich
A: plusx.de - agentur für kommunikation M: stefan@plusx.de

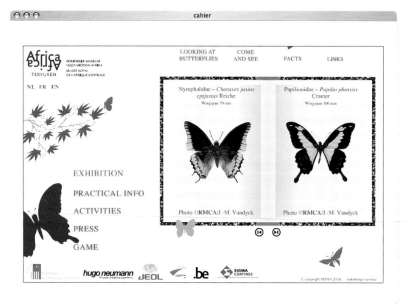

butterflies.africamuseum.be
D: fred vandenbreede C: olivier leemans P: laurent duffaut
A: so nice M: info@sonice.be

www.kotekom.com
D: kotékom
A: agence kotékom M: contact@kotekom.com

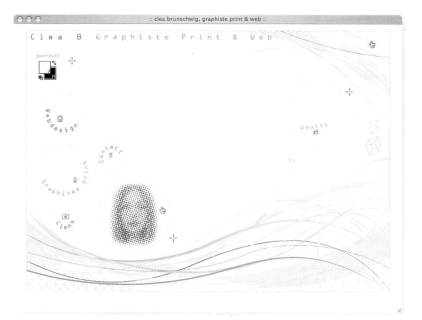

clea-b.com
D: clea brunschwig
A: clea b M: clea.brunschwig@wanadoo.fr

www.eisforeffort.com
D: rob young C: jason frinchaboy
A: effort M: rob@eisforeffort.com

www.grapa.ws
D: ferran pruneda, edgar seonae C: edgar seoane P: ferran pruneda
A: grapa.ws M: info@grapa.ws

www.herault-arnod.fr
D: eric leprince C: chris gaillard
A: herault arnod architectes M: chris@chrisgaillard.com

www.maritbeyer.de
D: maren prokopowitsch
M: mail@prokopowitsch.de

www.squidfire.com
D: owen linton C: owen linton P: jean-baptiste regnard
A: squidfire, inc. M: jbr@squidfire.com

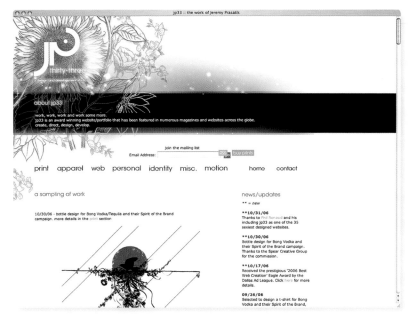

www.jp33.com
D: jeremy prasatik C: jeremy prasatik P: jeremy prasatik
A: jp33 - design and development M: me@jp33.com

www.nanhandbags.com
D: caroline king C: juliann wheeler P: julia abelmann
A: crown jules design M: nancy@nanhandbags.com

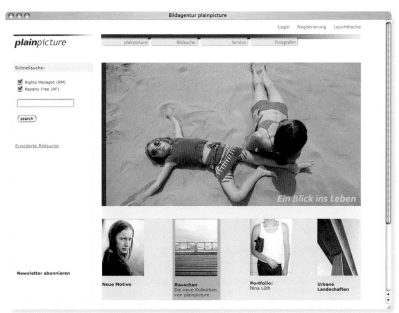

plainpicture.de
D: astrid herrmann C: benjamin vetter
A: plainpicture M: info@plainpicture.de

www.013a.com
D: matei apostolescu, karan singh C: karan singh P: matei apostolescu, karan singh
A: 013a M: mateiapostolescu@gmail.com

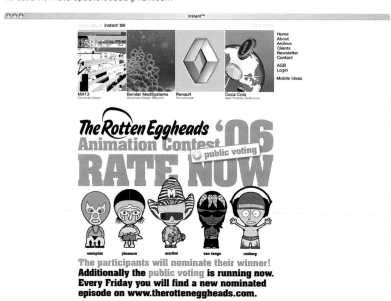

www.instant.at
D: gerald koeltringer C: instant, design gmbh P: instant, design gmbh
A: instant, design gmbh M: office@instant.at

www.lysergid.com
D: loïc sattler C: loïc sattler
M: contact@lysergid.com

couscouskid.co.uk
D: mathew star thomas
A: couscous kid M: mat@couscouskid.co.uk

www.lutz-jakubowski.de
D: matthias klegraf C: matthias klegraf P: sevn koeln
A: sevn koeln M: info@sevn.de

www.golibersuch.com
D: pete golibersuch C: pete golibersuch
A: golibersuch.com M: design@golibersuch.com

coudal.com
D: jim coudal
A: coudal partners inc. M: info@coudal.com

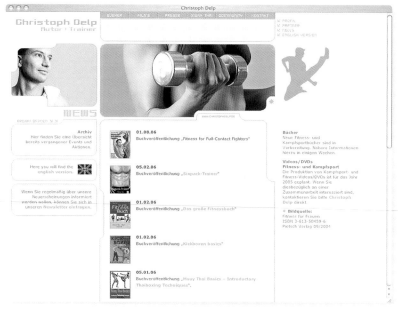

www.christophdelp.de
D: joachim schmidt C: joachim schmidt P: joachim schmidt
A: netztreu# M: www.netztreu.de

www.mywot.com
D: h. seppälä, v. kolehmainen C: kolehmainen, a. kokkonen P: kolehmainen, j. malviniemi
A: design agency fusion ltd. M: info@fusion.fi

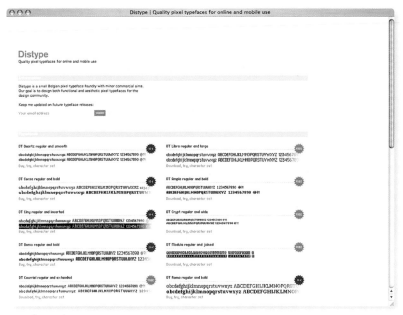

www.distype.be
D: nicolas deslé C: nicolas deslé P: nicolas deslé
A: dislogic M: info@dislogic.be

www.elektrischer-reporter.de
D: ralf graf
A: das-netzbuch.de, sixtus.net, handelsblatt.com M: post@elektrischer-reporter.de

www.convoice.it
D: andrea basile C: basile advertising, get solutions P: basile advertising
A: basile advertising M: info@basileadvertising.com

www.cookingstore.it
D: ilaria boz C: maurizio albertoni P: dps srl
A: dps srl M: i.boz@dpsonline.it

www.widsets.com
D: jani flink, sami koskela C: tuomas artman, juha toronen P: sami pekkola
A: valve M: press@widsets.com

www.thecabrians.com
D: david sánchez fernández C: rubén sánchez fernández
A: subculturaldesign M: ruben@factorianorte.com

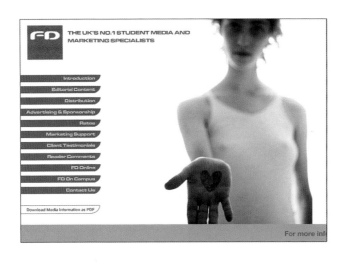

www.fd-media.co.uk
D: headchannel
M: info@headchannel.net

www.dizynotip.be
D: manuel piton C: manuel piton P: manuel piton
A: dizynotip M: manouel642@hotmail.com

www.merchandisem.com
D: marc alongina C: marc alongina P: anna guix
A: merchandise management M: mm@merchandisem.com

www.thorns.no/ltd/
D: håvard gjelseth, halvor bodin C: håvard gjelseth P: håvard gjelseth
A: this way design M: hgjelseth@thiswaydesign.com

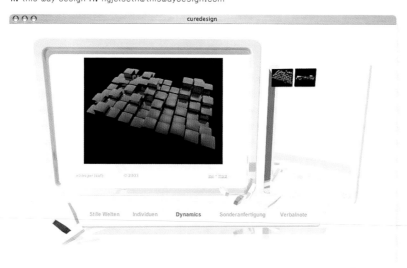

www.curedesign.de
D: sebastian künzel
A: curedesign M: sk@curedesign.de

www.pacdesco.com
D: marc a. ebalaroza, roy a. ebalaroza C: marc a. ebalaroza P: carl q. angel
A: pacdesco | pacdesco´s design community M: pacdesco@gmail.com

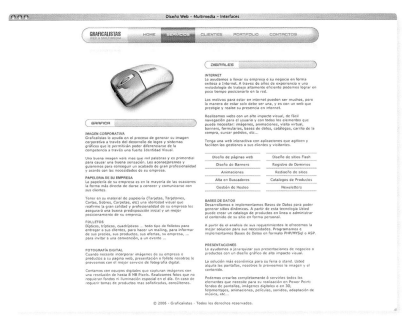

www.graficalistas.com.ar
D: andy clotta, gabi mariaca C: andy clotta P: andy clotta, gabi mariaca
A: www.graficalistas.com.ar M: info@graficalistas.com.ar

www.basileadvertising.com
D: andrea basile C: basile advertising, get solutions P: basile advertising
A: basile advertising M: info@basileadvertising.com

www.nameless.co.uk
D: adam millington C: rob hardwick, simon holliday, stewart morgan P: stuart gallemore
A: nameless media group ltd M: enquiries@nameless.co.uk

www.findeglueck.com
D: uwe bermeitinger C: mathias weitbrecht P: uwe bermeitinger
A: findeglueck imagekultivierung M: info@findeglueck.com

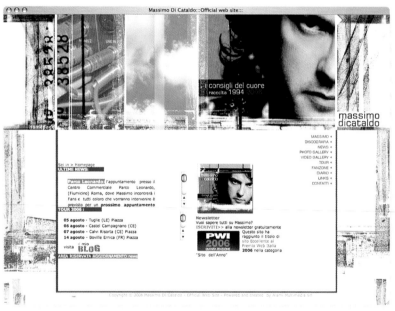

www.massimodicataldo.it
D: anna laura millacci C: anna laura millacci P: dicamusica srl
A: alami multimedia srl M: info@alamimultimedia.com

www.bombplacard.com
D: selcuk safci, murat canbaz C: gokhan okur P: d4d
A: d4d digital brand solutions M: info@d4d.com.tr

www.typografie.de
D: matthias ballmann
M: info@typografie.de

www.oralfix.com
D: jonathan harris
A: number 27 M: jjh@number27.org

www.escs.ipl.pt
D: abreu, rodrigues, santos C: estanqueiro, mimoso P: sendin, souto, moutinho, sousa
A: escola superior de comunicação social M: website@escs.ipl.pt

trippen

Kids

Children's version of the adult style with the same name. Lined with sheepskin lining all the way to the top.

♀ Dragon
Leather pub
Colours on request
Sizes 23-34

Order

www.trippen.com
D: v+i+s+k büro für visuelle kommunikation C: amt für gestaltung P: amt für gestaltung
A: v+i+s+k büro für visuelle kommunikation M: willkommen@v-i-s-k.de

www.dreamteambcn.com
D: jacinto lana C: jacinto lana P: jacinto lana
A: media.masmac.com M: jacinto@masmac.com

www.elequipoe.com
D: carolina alcalá C: francisco de casa P: jose manuel vega
A: el equipo e M: jmv@elequipoe.con

www.missyhaily.com
D: ilaria ranauro
M: missyhaily@gmail.com

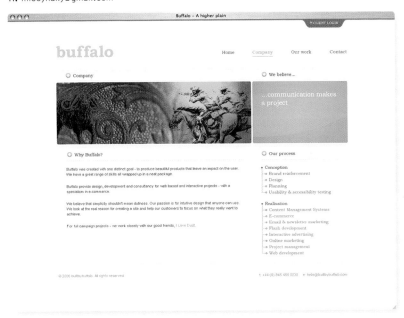

www.builtbybuffalo.com
D: jason reynolds C: nick stacey P: dan griffiths
A: buffalo M: hello@builtbybuffalo.com

www.infoavan.com
D: carlos esteban C: carlos esteban P: carlos esteban
A: infoavan M: snowave@gmail.com

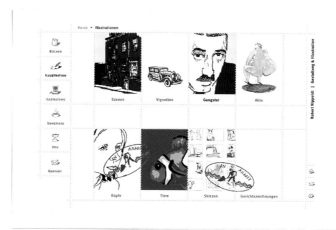

www.nippoldt.de
D: robert nippoldt
A: robert nippoldt | gestaltung und illustration M: robert@nippoldt.de

www.sweetsour.de
D: saskia müller C: nail yurtcu P: nail yurtcu
A: comstrate M: saskia.mueller.com

www.ideastep.com
D: ercan caliskan
A: ideastep M: ercan@ideastep.com

www.hmp-heidenhain.eu
D: manuel radde C: felix wittig P: bernd krause
A: designhaus berlin M: office@designhaus-berlin.de

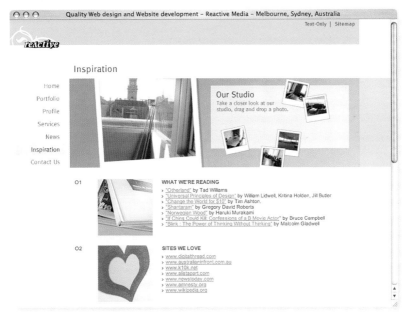

www.reactive.com
D: abby kelly C: ross richard, julian gilchrist P: tim o´neill, tim fouhy
A: reactive media M: chrisf@reactive.com

www.clubtransmediale.de
D: jan rohlf C: stefan schreck P: disk / club transmediale gbr
A: disk / club transmediale gbr M: postbox@clubtransmediale.de

www.gaston-lemme.de
D: axel becker C: stefan hermann P: axel becker
A: fortytwo-grafik design M: www.fortytwo.de

www.dexdesign.com.br
D: ricardo dexheimer C: ricardo dexheimer P: ricardo dexheimer
A: dex M: contato@dexdesign.com.br

www.rasikarestaurant.com
D: cristian strittmatter C: gabriel toledano P: sandra strittmatter
A: from scratch design studio M: contact@fromscratch.us

www.heroexports.com
D: kushal grover P: pugmarks
A: liquid designs india M: www.liquiddesignsindia.com

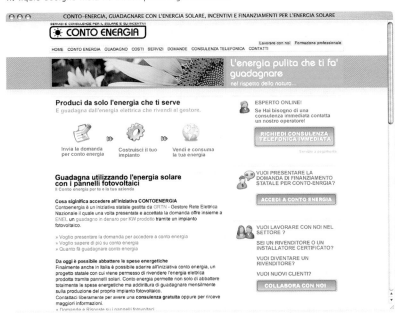

www.conto-energia.biz
D: gabriele stampa C: gianluca bau P: medialinx srl
A: medialinx srl M: info@medialinx.it

www.funbox.com.tw/ezlife/flipflap
D: liao mu wei P: liao mu wei
A: funbox studio M: wingerliao@pchome.com.tw

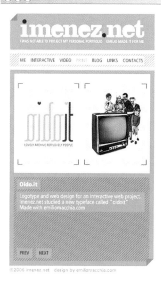

www.imenez.net
D: irene bacchi, emilio macchia C: emilio macchia P: irene bacchi
A: imenez.net M: irene@imenez.net

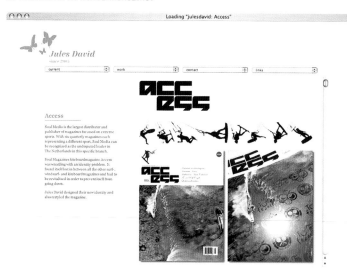

www.julesdavid.com
D: julien david rademaker
A: jules david M: julien@julesdavid.com

www.chicago-zone.net
D: chollier guillaume C: chollier guillaume P: chollier guillaume
A: look on web M: www.lookonweb.fr

YOUR WEEK WITH US

Our cooking courses are very hands-on. They are taught in English, but you will acquire a smattering of culinary Italian. Local chefs will guide you through the preparation of simple but delicious dishes (from Tuscany and from other Italian regions) and reveal some of their culinary secrets. Groups are small (maximum 8 people), so that everyone gets a chance to try their hand at every technique, from making fresh egg pasta dough to lovingly stirring an artichoke risotto to perfection.

You are free to pick and choose whether you'd like to join in the cookery holiday activities on a particular day or not. If you fancy a day horse-riding, hot-air ballooning or just going to the beach, let us know and we'll help you do just that. Car hire is essential so that you can explore the area on your own, and tailor the cooking vacation programme to your wishes.

Here is a typical week at Organic Tuscany:

SATURDAY

You arrive
We help you get settled in to your apartment by leaving you a basket filled with organic goodies – fruit, honey, coffee and biscuits.
Have a dip in the pool or an exploratory hike (we provide a hiking map of the area).

8.30 pm
Alfresco welcome dinner at our home, La Selva, where the cooking courses will be held.
We light the wood-fired oven and you assemble your own pizza and foccaccia, to go with grilled organic vegetables and crisp salads, all washed down with local biodynamic wine.

A VEGETABLE LOVER'S PARADISE

With its great variety of fresh fruit and vegetables, as well as cereals that are little used elsewhere, Italian food affords a host of exquisite flavours for vegetarians. The traditional "peasant" food of Tuscany is no exception: nutty pulses, tangy vegetable sauces and imaginative salads all have an important part to play on the Organic Tuscany table. Two of the cooking courses we offer are entirely vegetarian.

We share the ever-growing concerns about pesticide residues and GM foods. In the vast majority of cases, the ingredients we use are organic or biodynamic. All are fresh and locally produced. We take you to see the organic farms where the ingredients that we cook with are grown, such as cereals, vegetables and olive oil. We visit the vineyards where the biodynamic wine we drink is produced.

www.organictuscany.org
D: riccardo piattelli C: riccardo piattelli P: shilpa baliga
A: piattelli design M: riccardo@riccardo.net

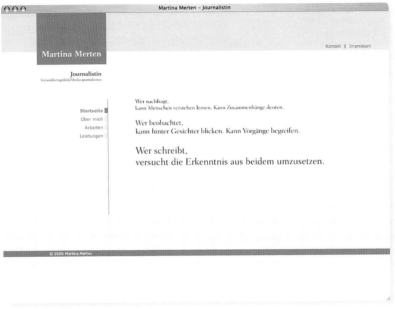

www.martina-merten.de
D: andrea podbevsek C: andrea podbevsek, gerrick kammholz P: pixelbasis.
A: pixelbasis. M: info@martina-merten.de

www.ifdep.pt
D: filipe cavaco, alexandre r. gomes C: alexandre r. gomes, gws P: gws
A: gws M: alex@burocratik.com

BERNHARD WOLFF

Startseite
Leistungen Und
Angebot
Biografie
Termine
Kontakt und
Impressum

Bernhard Wolff ist ...

✓ Rückwärtssprecher

✓ Entertainer

✓ Moderator

✓ Konzeptioner

✓ Trainer

» mehr Informationen

Die nächsten Termine

Bernhard Wolff ist mit seinem Programm „Denken hilft!" an folgenden Terminen zu sehen:

22. - Berlin, Kookaburra-Club
25.2.06

22.03.06 Mannheim, Landesmuseum für Technik und Arbeit

23. - Hamburg, Quatsch
26.03.06 Comedy Club

» Weitere Termine

Die Solo-Show

Denken hilft
die Show zum schlauer machen

Bernhard Wolff präsentiert seine Soloshow „Denken hilft"

» Mehr Infos

Achtung Baustelle!

Informationen für Sie
Die Homepage von Bernhard Wolff befindet sich im Aufbau. Bis zum Jahreswechsel informieren wir Sie hier nur kurz und knapp.

Kontakt und Beratung
Booking Theater: Vanessa de Boer
Tel. 040/414290-31
» E-Mail senden

Booking Events: Sebastian Dornemann
Tel. 040/414290-30
» E-Mail senden

Multitalent

Bernhard Wolff ist Moderator, Entertainer und Trainer. Der Wirtschaftspädagoge und Gründer des Think-Theatre hat sich auf intelligente Live-Kommunikation spezialisiert – für Tagungen, Events und Messen. Als Infotainer und Gastredner sind seine Themen Denken und Gehirn, Gedächtnis und Kommunikation. Wolffs Spezialität ist das „Rückwärtssprechen" – mit Auftritten in über 30 TV-Shows. Am 15.10.2005 ist die Premiere seiner ersten Soloshow „Denken hilft" in der Alten Mühle in Bad Vilbel.

Links
Besuchen Sie auch die Partner-Websites von Bernhard Wolff.

» Wolff tritt gegen...
» Think-Theater

www.bernhard-wolff.de
D: jan persiel C: jan persiel P: jan persiel
A: schoengeist.de M: www.schoengeist.de

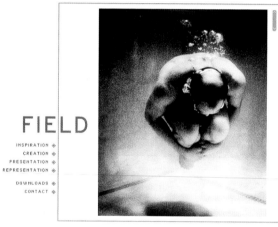

FIELD

INSPIRATION ✦
CREATION ✦
PRESENTATION ✦
REPRESENTATION ✦

DOWNLOADS ✦
CONTACT ✦

◈ FIELD MEDIA PRACTICE

www.fieldmediapractice.com
D: anton bensdorp C: ron valstar
A: ultrafris M: info@ultrafris.nl

www.gharnatatours.com.ly
D: khairy mohamed shaban C: khairy mohamed shaban P: khairy mohamed shaban
A: gharnatatours M: khairy@lttnet.net

www.oceanic.com.fj
D: maria ronna luna pastorizo P: jonathan segal
A: oceanic communications, fiji islands M: info@oceanic.com.fj

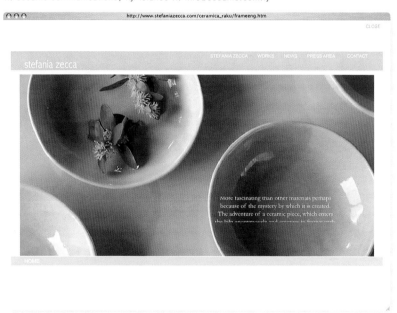

www.stefaniazecca.com
D: massimiliano rossi
A: rossi comunicazione M: info@massimilianorossi.it

www.pusch-partner.net
D: stefan hintermeier C: andreas hintermeier P: daniel rousta
A: h2r media solutions | hintermeier, rousta gbr M: www.h2r-mediasolutions.de

www.davidbarcos.com
D: joseba ares bermejo, jorge edwards gutiérrez C: j. a. bermejo P: ecequiel barricart
A: you media M: joseba@youmedia.es

www.dieseitenmacher.at
D: philipp steinkellner C: philipp steinkellner P: stefan olbrich
A: die seitenmacher internet-agentur M: s.olbrich@dieseitenmacher.at

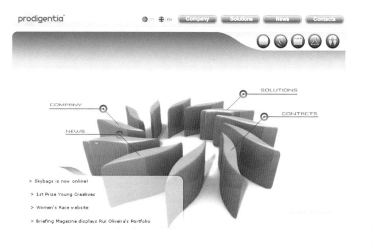

prodigentia.com
D: carlos sampaio, jignehs manmohandas, rui oliveira C: diogo antunes, luis domingues
A: prodigentia M: info@prodigentia.com

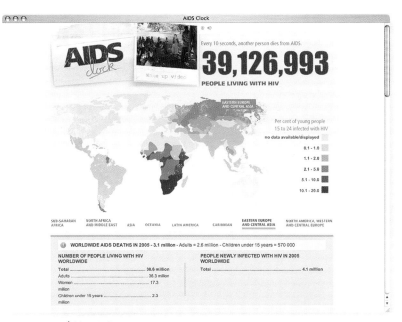

www.unfpa.org/aids_clock
D: allysson lucca **P:** alvaro serrano
A: unfpa - united nations population fund **M:** serrano@unfpa.org

www.echochoice.de
D: ralf strasner **C:** florian steinig **P:** echochoice medialab
A: echochoice medialab **M:** info@echochoice.de

www.positiff.ru
D: george yefremoff **C:** alexander dorodnoff **P:** george yefremoff
A: positiff **M:** www.positiff.ru

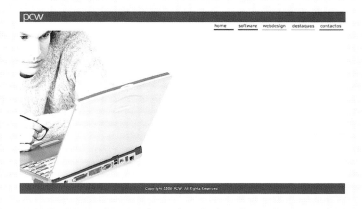

www.pcw.pt
D: paula granja C: paula granja P: paula granja
A: pcw M: paulagranja@pcw.pt

www.chateauroux.co.uk
D: nick raven C: two design (flash) look-systems (e-commerce) P: greg white
A: chateau roux M: info@twodesign.co.uk & website@chateauroux.co.uk

www.hopkingdesign.com
D: mez hopking C: mez hopking
A: hopking design M: mez@hopkingdesign.com

100

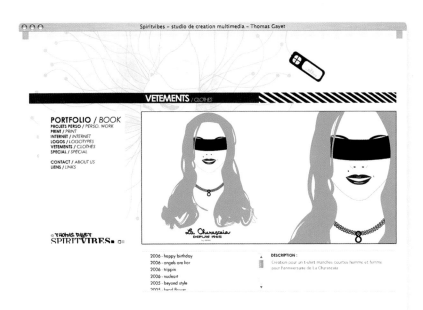

www.spiritvibes.com
D: thomas gayet C: jean charles hoffmann P: thomas gayet
A: spiritvibes M: tg@spiritvibes.com

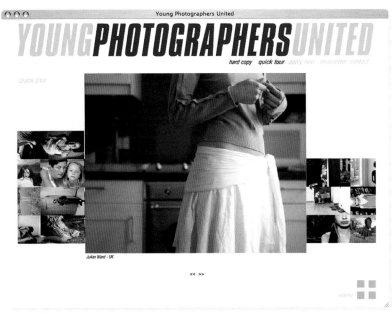

ypu.org
D: wim lauwers C: thomas de groote P: chris de backer
A: woowoos nv M: info@woowoos.com

www.sanfil.pt
D: cristiano teixeira C: cristiano teixeira P: andreia dias
A: alperce, serviços web M: contactos@alperce.com

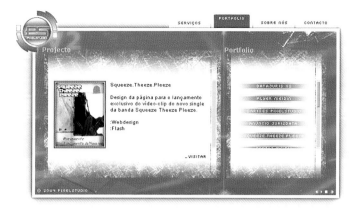

www.pixelstudio.info
D: rui simões C: isac pinto P: rui simões
A: pixelstudio M: info@pixelstudio.info

www.magic-sandwich.co.uk
D: kevin stone
A: magic sandwich M: kevvstone@hotmail.com

www.notariat-rathausmarkt.de
D: dirk heinemann C: henning lehfeldt P: anke rippert
A: nordisch.com M: dirk.heinemann@nordisch.com

www.northwestdesign.net
D: paul hailing C: thomas olsen P: paul hailing
A: www.northwestdesign.net M: ph@northwestdesign.net

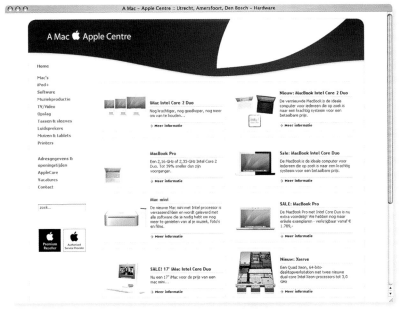

www.a-mac.nl
D: t. muusers C: t. muusers, p.a.h. meeuwsen P: t. muusers
A: vak18 M: info@vak18.com

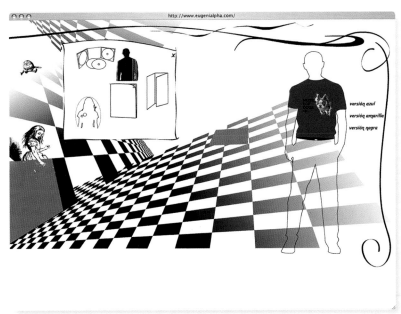

www.eugenialpha.com
D: eugenia garrido
M: contacta@eugenialpha.com

www.teyco.es
D: ignacio zorraquín P: ona lab
A: nomadesign M: www.nomadesign.org

www.coordination-berlin.de
D: coordination berlin
A: coordination berlin M: mail@coordination-berlin.de

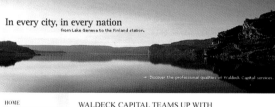

www.waldeckcapital.com/index.shtml
D: radek vasicek P: thomas smit
A: radekvasicek.com M: info@radekvasicek.com

104

www.hersteragarden.com
D: andreas hagemann C: daniel kremin
A: hagemannplus M: www.hagemannplus.de

www.geocities.com/b_zippor/something2.htm
D: boaz zippor C: boaz zippor
M: boaz@boazzippor.net

www.matiasavila.com
D: matias avila
A: avila diseño M: info@matiasavila.com

www.festivaldenkbeeldig.nl
D: sander crombach P: tim schellekens
A: studio jan koek M: info@studiojankoek.nl

dolceq.com
D: massimiliano panzironi C: massimiliano panzironi P: m. panzironi, sonia di rubbo
A: dolceq M: info@dolceq.com

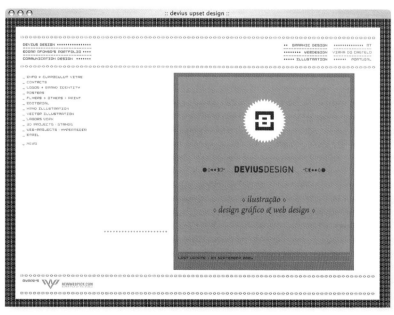

www.deviusdesign.com
D: edgar afonso C: edgar afonso P: edgar afonso
A: deviusdesign M: edgar@deviusdesign.com

www.mantado.com
D: oliver warren C: oliver warren P: john galloway
A: mantado M: john@mantado.com

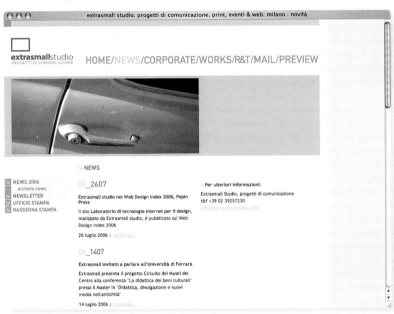

www.extrasmallstudio.com
D: letizia bollini C: criticalbit
A: extrasmall studio M: www.extrasmallstudio.com

www.ofmecc.com
D: clara porta
A: digitalfog M: webdesign@digitalfog.it

This is my art.

Bye bye.

www.hellohello.name
D: stephen crowhurst C: stephen crowhurst P: stephen crowhurst
A: hello hello M: steph@hellohello.name

java

JAVA COMMUNICATIONS HAS BEEN LEAVING ITS INDELIBLE MARK ON
DESIGN, ADVERTISING, MULTIMEDIA, MARKETING AND COPYWRITING EVER
SINCE ITS INCEPTION IN 1991. [STRATEGIC PLANNING. DELIVERING ON
SCHEDULE. ACTIVE LISTENING. TAMING INSANE DEADLINES. DISCIPLINE +
RIGOUR. PASSION + CREATIVITY. DRIVE. BLISS. RESEARCH. COMPULSIVE HI
TECH JARGON LITERACY. IMAGINATION IN SPADES. SOLUTIONS.]

PRINT
MULTIMEDIA
MISSION
TEAM
REACH US
FRANÇAIS

www.javacom.qc.ca
D: philippe roy C: philippe roy
A: 1l 2p M: phil@un1deuxp.com

www.charitomuchamarcha.com
D: abraham vivas C: abraham vivas P: abraham vivas
A: charito mucha marcha M: info@charitomuchamarcha.com

108

www.brija.com
D: goran grudic
A: gruda designs M: admin@brija.com

www.ivisual.it
D: daniele lodi rizzini C: daniele giusti P: daniele lodi rizzini
A: segno&forma M: info@segnoeforma.it

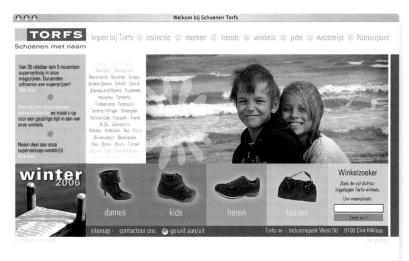

www.torfs.be
D: gerda van damme C: guido janssens
A: dreammachine M: info@dreammachine.be

www.id-k.com
D: gregory gasser, michael ziska C: g. gasser, m. ziska P: id-k kommunikationsdesign
A: id-k kommunikationsdesign M: info@id-k.com

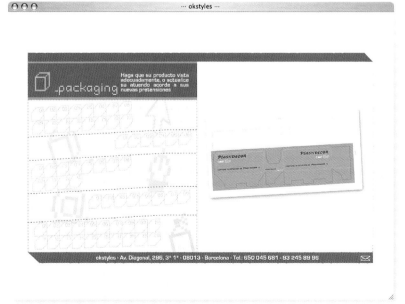

www.arcanoah.com
D: rocky
A: arca noah communication design M: info@arcanoah.com

www.okstyles.com
D: victor garcia alvarez C: victor garcia alvarez P: victor garcia alvarez
A: okstyles M: info@okstyles.com

thelaunderette.com
D: john white C: avenue P: avenue
A: avenue M: hello@thelaunderette.com

www.enginecreative.co.uk
D: andy wise, matthew key C: james gardner P: andy wise, matthew key,
A: engine M: hello@enginecreative.co.uk

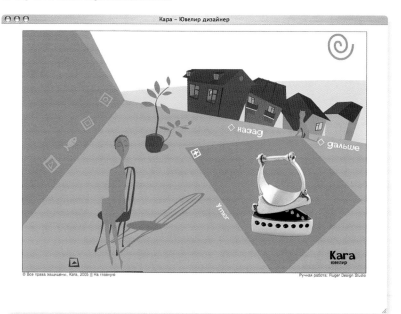

www.kara.am
D: aghasi aghabalyan C: andrey vanyan P: aghasi aghabalyan
A: fluger M: fluger@fluger.com

www.azuldecorso.com.ar
D: azul de corso C: diego gimenez P: azul de corso
A: azul de corso M: hello@azuldecorso.com.ar

www.buzzlogic.com
D: shawn click C: jean bigras P: tushar atre
A: atrenet M: atre.net

pinballdrive.com
D: yu koyanagi C: yu koyanagi P: yu koyanagi
A: yours store M: you@yours-store.com

112

www.cnscomunicazione.com
D: andrea orazzo C: andrea orazzo P: cns comunicazione
A: cns comunicazione M: andrea@andreaorazzo.com

www.kamiprofumi.it
D: laura barbera, alessandro demicheli C: nicola destefano
A: carsons & co M: a.demicheli@carsons.it

www.design-werk.org
D: wolfram söll C: wolfram söll
A: designwerk M: w.soell@t-online.de

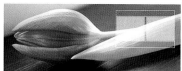

www.2nddesign.net
D: oliver schmid C: oliver schmid P: oliver schmid
A: webgarten gmbh M: oliver.schmid@webgarten.ch

www.nigeltomm.com
D: algirdas javtokas C: algirdas javtokas P: nigel tomm
A: ppuppy design clinic M: algirdas.javtokas@nigeltomm.com

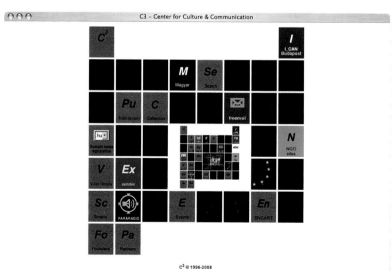

www.c3.hu
D: balázs beöthy C: gusztáv nikázy P: c3 center for culture and communication
M: info@c3.hu

www.designers-skulls.de
D: ekkehard beck, lutz härer, michael heß C: ekkehard beck, michael heß P: ekkehard beck
A: designers skulls M: head@designers-skulls.de

www.rogerblack.com
D: roger black, rob hunter C: jonathan raftery, rob hunter P: rob hunter
A: roger black studio, inc. M: tips@rogerblack.com

amplitudecerta.pt
D: ana abreu
A: cores ao cubo - gabinete de design M: info@coresaocubo.pt

www.digraph.it
D: elisa gennari C: elisa gennari
A: gap studio instaff communication network, elisir design M: info@instaff.org

www.multimediamakers.be
D: els van de veire C: els van de veire P: els van de veire
A: multimediamakers M: els.vandeveire@multimediamakers.be

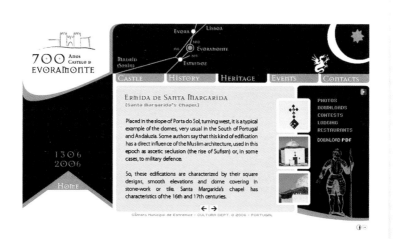

www.castelodevoramonte.com
D: paula moreira, pedro calhordas C: p moreira, p. calhordas P: camara municipal estremoz
A: pedro calhordas M: pedro@calhordas.com

116

www.rothaniko.hu
D: kilfish
M: kilfish@kilfish.pardey.org

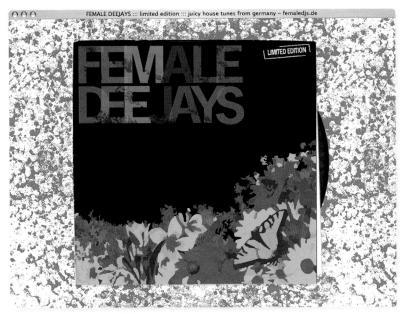

www.femaledjs.de
D: jan weiss C: jan weiss
A: kreativkopf.tv M: www.kreativkopf.tv

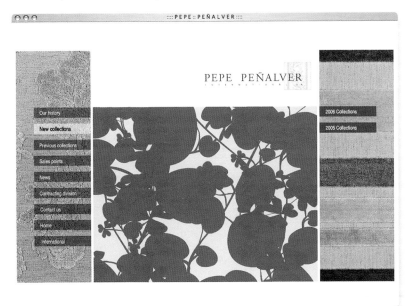

www.pepepenalver.com
D: pepe cruz novillo C: rafael martínez P: rafael martínez
A: www.fabricanet.com M: rafael@fabricanet.com

www.shiloo.de
D: stefan schröder C: stefan schröder
M: house8@gmx.de

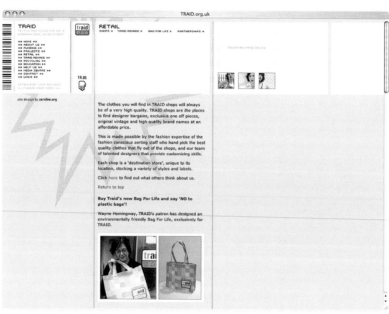

www.traid.org.uk
D: paul buck, ela kosmaczewska, zerofee
A: textile recycling for aid and international development M: info@traid.org.uk

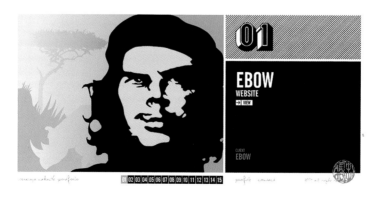

www.masayanakade.com
D: masaya nakade
M: m_nakade@hotmail.com

www.mochikit.com
D: ian main, josh pigford C: bob ippolito P: ryan nichols, jameson hsu
A: apples to oranges, mochi media M: info@mochimedia.com

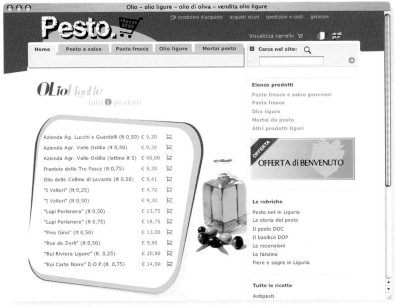

www.pesto.net
D: ilaria boz, mara musso
A: village srl M: ila74@libero.it

www.heymannn.de/home.htm
D: nicolai heymann
M: nicolai@heymannn.de

www.falco.sk
D: viktor kovac
A: g31d.com creative agency **M:** info@g31d.com

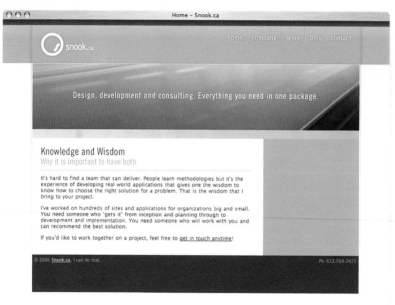

www.snook.ca
D: chris murphy **C:** jonathan snook
A: snook.ca web development inc. **M:** jonathan@snook.ca

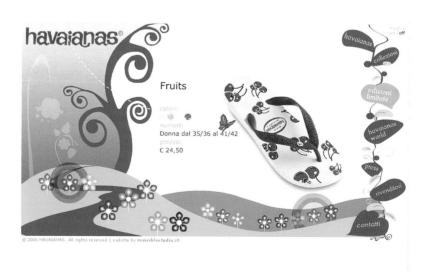

www.havaianas.it
D: stefania boiano **P:** regina regis
A: invisiblestudio **M:** www.invisiblestudio.it

www.pestridge.com
D: tim pestridge
A: tim pestridge photography & design M: studio@pestridge.com

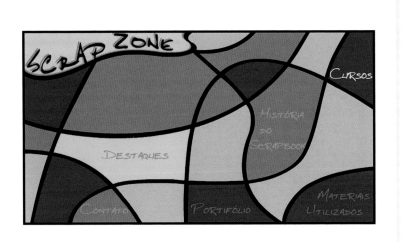

www.scrapzone.com.br
D: fernanda filippini, danielle liz pietrocolla C: f. filippini P: danielle pietrocolla
A: scrapzone M: fernanda@filippini.com.br

www.weverling.nl
D: boy brabander
A: bleu rivage M: rjonge@weverling.nl

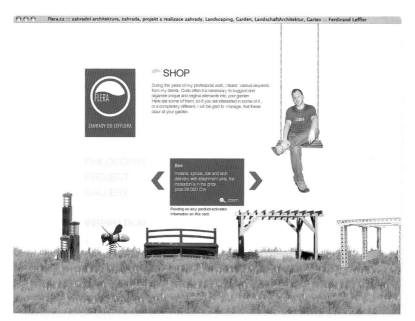

www.flera.cz
D: mireque kodesh C: mireque kodesh
A: studio klubismus M: studio@klubismus.cz

www.xeta.de
D: philip hohn C: nikolai stein-cieslak P: philip hohn
A: xeta. create. operate. M: info@xeta.de

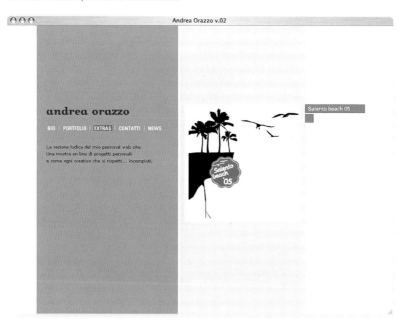

www.andreaorazzo.com
D: andrea orazzo
M: andrea@andreaorazzo.com

www.applinet.nl
D: debby van dongen C: rené pijlman, debby van dongen P: rené pijlman
A: conk M: www.conk.nl

www.new-media-agency.com
D: evgeniy spikhaylov C: sergey mitskevich P: maxim parovin
A: jidg, new media agency M: info@new-media-agency.com

www.blueeyesmagazine.com
D: chris vivion C: seth bro
A: blueeyes magazine M: chris@blueeyesmagazine.com

www.detalle.cl
D: fernanda garcia P: maria jesus martorell
A: nuestragencia M: www.nuestragencia.cl

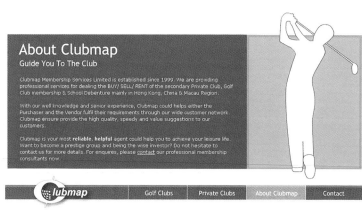

www.clubmap.com.hk
D: arnold chen C: arnold chen P: arnold chen
A: design 97 services company M: info@design97.com

www.wikiwi.be
D: de naeyer raphael C: de naeyer raphael P: de naeyer raphael
A: wikiwi.be M: info@wikiwi.be

www.farmpark.nl
D: jacco bogaerds C: jacco bogaerds P: jacco bogaerds
A: farmpark M: jacco@farmpark.nl

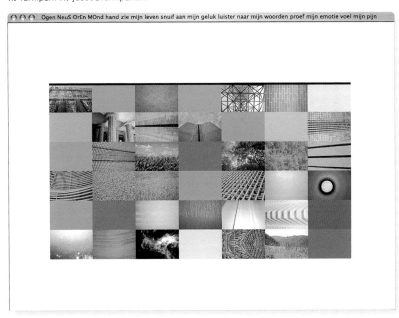

gedichten.webpunt.nl
D: p.j.h.m. hendrikx C: p.j.h.m. hendrikx P: p.j.h.m. hendrikx
A: webpunt.nl M: p.hendrikx@webpunt.nl

im.digitalhymn.com
D: davide casali C: davide casali P: davide casali
A: digitalhymn M: folletto@gmail.com

www.swissandfamous.ch
D: chris eggli C: marc rinderknecht
A: swissandfamous, kobebeef M: mr@kobebeef.ch

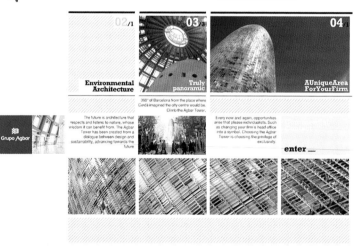

www.torreagbar.com
D: nuria reolid, olivier grau, m. martí C: j. álvarez, g. bayarri, v. sansano, a. botella
A: vis-tek.com M: www.vis-tek.com

www.azuloscurocasinegro.com
D: rafael martínez, ángel cano C: rafael martínez P: rafael martínez
A: hi creative M: www.fabricanet.com

www.villa-zeljka.com
D: veljko sekelj C: matija tomaskovic P: veljko sekelj
A: evolva M: info@evolva.hr

www.emiliopenya.com
D: emilio josé peñaranda garcía C: emilio josé peñaranda garcía
A: emilio peña M: info@emiliopenya.com

www.kctarifa.com
D: gamonoso C: madden P: gamonoso
A: gamonoso*graphics M: www.gamonoso.com

www.eendar.com
D: mónica calvo C: carlos rincon P: mónica calvo
A: organicfields M: monica@organicfields.net

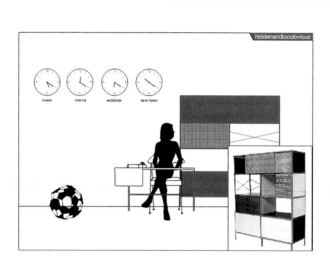

www.hiddenandtooobvious.com
D: stephane cauwel C: stephane cauwel
A: hiddenandtooobvious M: sc@hiddenandtooobvious.com

www.bufc.de
D: chris alt C: gregor braun P: snapdragon
M: design@chrisalt.com

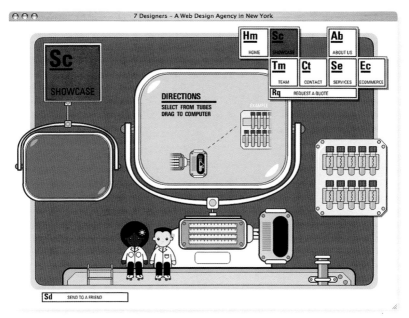

www.7designers.com
D: asi erenberg C: ziv marom P: asi erenberg
A: ecommerce partners M: info@7designers.com

www.miss-k.ch
D: karin estermann
M: miss@miss-k.ch

blog.nemstudio.com
D: michaël villar
M: michael@nemstudio.com

www.network-tr.com
D: selcuk safci C: murat canbaz P: d4d
A: d4d digital brand solutions M: info@d4d.com.tr

www.kilfish.com
D: kilfish
M: kilfish@kilfish.pardey.org

www.semente.net
D: pedro heitor, aiste martinaityte, vasco banza
M: apoio@semente.net

www.airforsoul.com
D: david ghelman
A: the inet group M: info@inetgroup.com

www.nexuscreative.com
D: peter wong C: peter wong P: peter wong
A: nexuscreative music & design M: nexus@nexuscreative.com

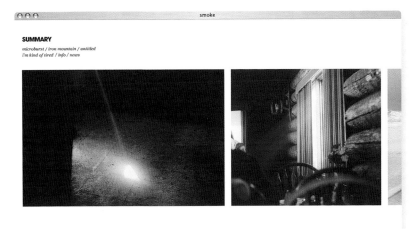

www.adambernales.com
D: adam bernales
A: seiche M: starelic@hotmail.com

www.vincent.durbak.sk
D: vincent durbak C: vincent durbak
M: vincent@durbak.sk

www.mooncruise.com
D: trevor brady C: aleksander katusenko, alfredo chu P: trevor brady
A: mooncruise* M: mooncruise@gmail.com

www.sonnenvogel.com
D: axel hebenstreit
A: sonnenvogel - atelier für gestaltung M: axel@sonnenvogel.com

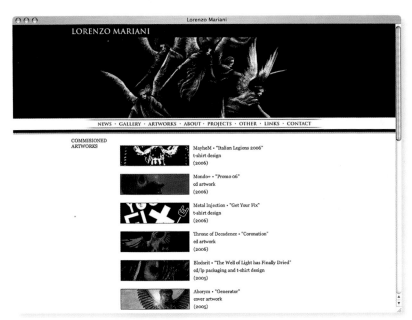

www.lorenzomariani.it
D: håvard gjelseth C: håvard gjelseth P: håvard gjelseth
A: this way design M: havardg@thiswaydesign.com

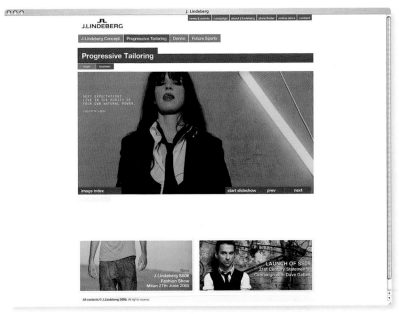

www.studiolam.com
D: jody work C: mike piacenza P: donna piacenza
A: studio 1a.m. M: whatnot@studiolam.com

www.jlindeberg.com
D: emil lanne, nico nuzzaci C: andrew knott, emil lanne P: lizzie underwood
A: poke M: www.pokelondon.com

www.anomali.se/
D: lars oldenburg C: lars oldenburg P: lars oldenburg
A: bokförlaget anomali M: lars@anomali.se

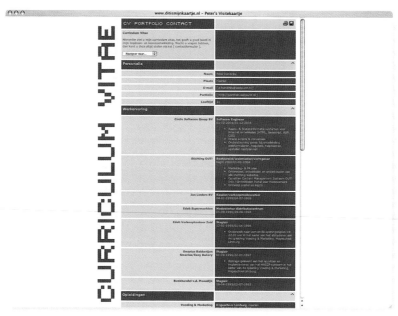

www.ditismijnkaartje.nl
D: p.j.h.m. hendrikx C: p.j.h.m. hendrikx P: p.j.h.m. hendrikx
A: webpunt.nl M: p.hendrikx@webpunt.nl

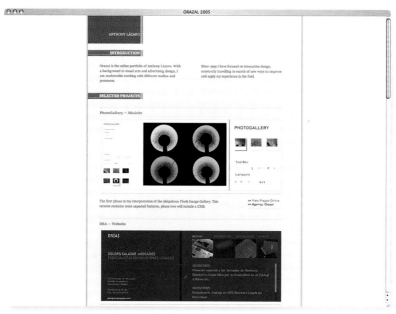

www.orazal.com
D: anthony lazaro
A: orazal M: lazaro@orazal.com

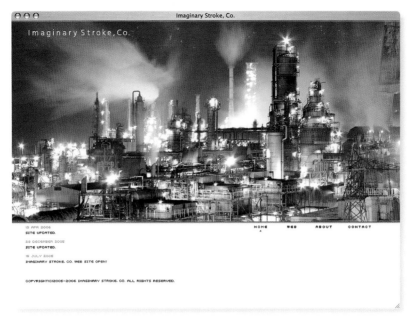

www.imaginarystroke.com
D: fumiaki hamagami C: fumiaki hamagami P: fumiaki hamagami
A: imaginary stroke, co M: isc@imaginarystroke.com

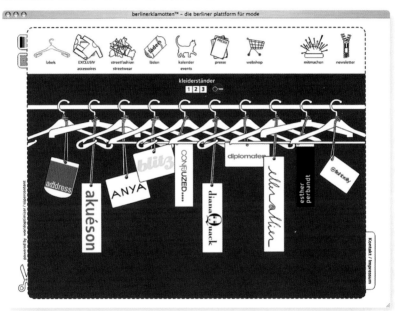

www.berlinerklamotten.de
D: eike wendland C: sandiipa ziebell, kevin proesel
A: worldoptimizer.com M: icke@worldoptimizer.com

www.luxury-creation.com
D: marcello vigoni C: flash 8 P: tls
A: tuninglove services M: www.tl-services.com

notcot.org
D: jean aw C: daniel frysinger
A: notcot inc. M: jaw@notcot.com

www.amkashop.com
D: thomas gayet C: jean charles hoffmann P: thomas gayet
A: spiritvibes, amkashop M: thomas@amkashop.com

www.w-dizajn.hr
D: tomislav katinic P: tomislav katinic
A: w-dizajn M: info@w-dizajn.hr

www.31three.com
D: jesse bennett-chamberlain
A: 31three M: jessebc@31three.com

www.pacogarciadj.com
D: emilio josé peñaranda garcía C: emilio josé peñaranda garcía P: paco garcía
A: emilio peña M: info@emiliopenya.com

www.faerie.fr
D: aurélien durand C: benoît germond
A: e-jdid M: aureliendurand@hotmail.com

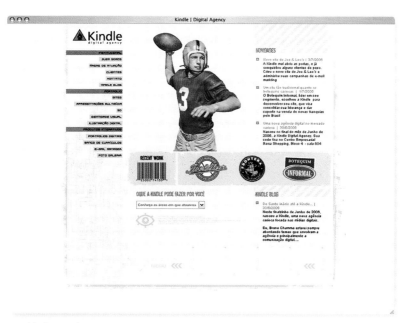

www.kindle.com.br
D: bruno chamma C: rodrigo albuquerque P: bruno magalhães
A: kindle digital agency M: chamma@kindle.com.br

www.socket-studios.co.uk
D: paul macgregor C: paul macgregor P: paul macgregor
A: socket studios M: paul@socket-studios.co.uk

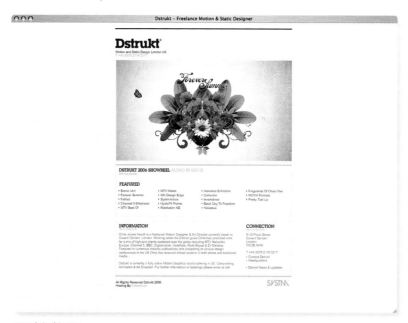

www.dstrukt.com
D: chris james hewitt C: chris james hewitt P: chris james hewitt
A: dstrukt M: chris@dstrukt.com

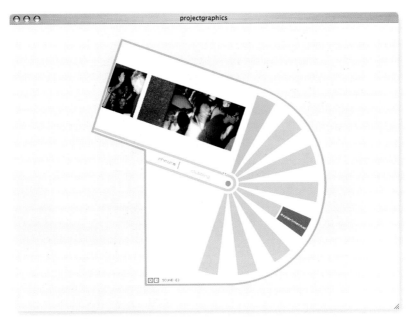

www.projectgraphics.net
D: agon çeta **C:** flakërim ismani
A: projectgraphics **M:** contact@projectgraphics.net

www.sirastudio.net
D: marc torrente cesteros **C:** marc torrente cesteros **P:** marc torrente cesteros
A: sirastudio **M:** info@sirastudio.net

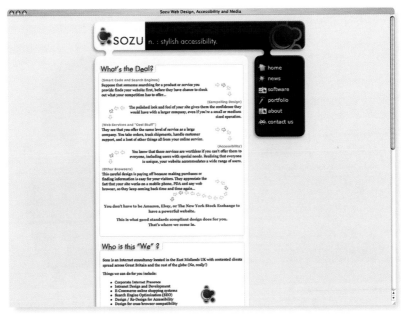

www.sozu.co.uk
D: denyer
A: sozu ltd **M:** enquiries@sozu.co.uk

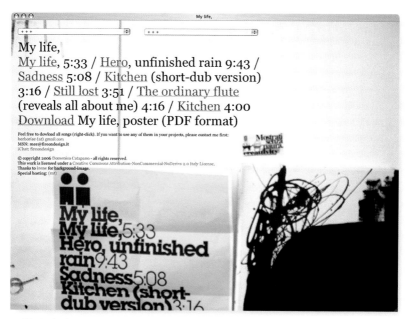

mylife.herborize.com
D: domenico catapano C: domenico catapano P: domenico catapano
A: herborize M: herborize@gmail.com

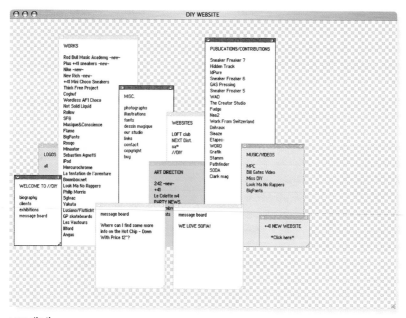

www.diy.li
D: diy C: gaël hugo P: diy
A: diy M: info@diy.li

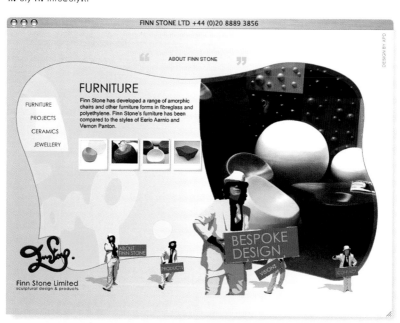

www.finnstone.com/flash.html
D: clemens hackl, grazia cantoni C: clemens hackl
A: exponential design ltd M: www.exponentialdesign.co.uk

www.paulantonson.com
D: paul antonson
M: pa@paulantonson.com

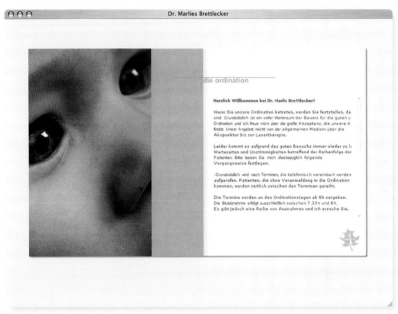

www.dr-brettlecker.at
D: dietmar halbauer, christof höglinger C: dietmar halbauer P: embers consulting, artworker
A: embers consulting gmbh M: d.halbauer@embers.at

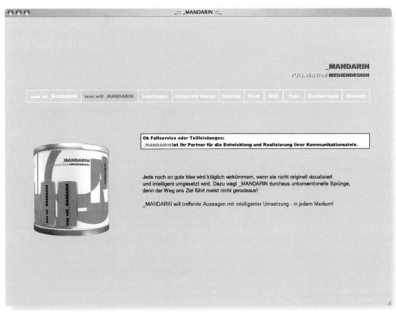

www.mandarindose.com
D: rene rothmann C: rene rothmann P: rene rothmann
A: mandarin M: mango@mandarindose.com

www.engine-productions.de
D: christian spatz C: jörn gahrmann P: engine-productions
A: engine-productions M: www.engine-productions.de

themediaco.com
D: roy husada C: alfredo chu, aleksander katusenko P: trevor brady
A: themedia M: info@themediaco.com

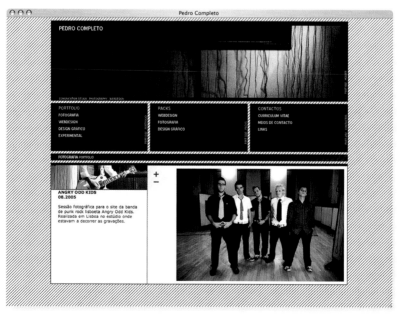

pedrocompleto.no.sapo.pt
D: pedro completo
M: p.completo@sapo.pt

www.linda-gefuehle.de
D: stefan hansel C: stefan hansel P: stefan hansel
M: design@linda-gefuehle.de

www.aftercode.com
D: claudio naboni
M: info@aftercode.com

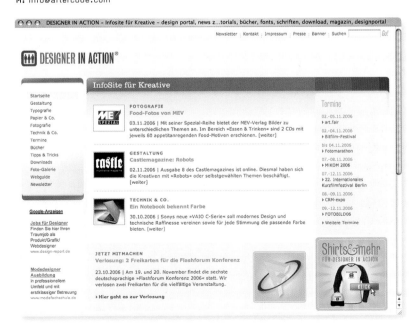

www.designerinaction.de
D: marco rullkötter, dirk rullkötter C: marco rullkötter P: marco rullkötter
A: marco rullkötter agd M: info@designerinaction.de

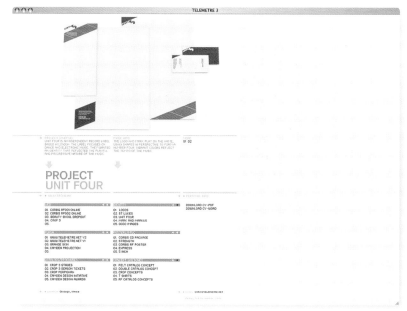

www.telemetre.net
D: chris may C: chris may P: chris may
A: telemetre M: chris@telemetre.net

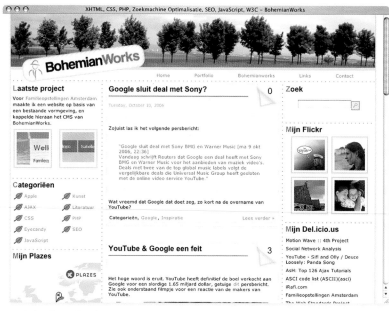

www.bohemianworks.nl
D: jeroen hulscher C: jeroen hulscher P: jeroen hulscher
A: bohemianworks M: info@bohemianworks.nl

www.juanito.com.br
D: joão paulo teixeira
A: midiaweb M: joaopaulots@gmail.com

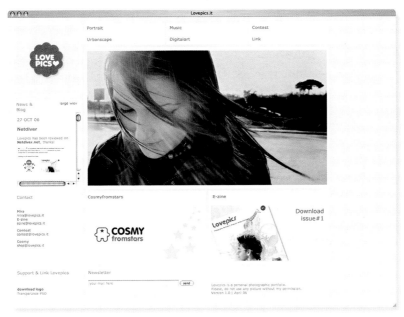

www.lovepics.it
D: michela 'mira' rapacciuolo C: michela 'mira' rapacciuolo P: michela 'mira' rapacciuolo
A: lovepics M: mira@lovepics.it

honeyeatyoursalad.org
D: jesse kanda C: jesse kanda P: jesse kanda
A: honey eat your salad M: jesse@humili.com

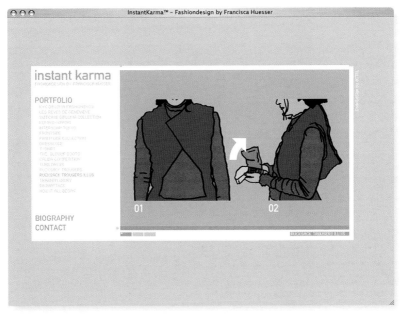

www.instant-karma.ch
D: andreas lorenz C: andreas lorenz P: andreas lorenz, francisca hüsser
A: dctrl - interactive media & motion graphics gmbh M: info@dctrl.com

www.komfortabel.ch
D: gregory gasser C: gregory gasser, benjamin nyffenegger P: id-k.com
A: id-k kommunikationsdesign M: g.gasser@id-k.com

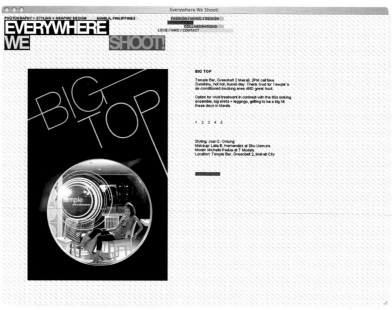

www.everywhereweshoot.com
D: ryan inigo vergara, garovs garrovillo C: everywhere we shoot! P: everywhere we shoot!
A: everywhere we shoot! M: info@everywhereweshoot.com

www.agraph.be
D: olivier leemans C: olivier leemans P: olivier leemans
A: @graph M: info@agraph.be

146

www.studiomom.nl
D: aad krol (vivid), alfred van elk, mars holwerda (studiomom) **C:** aad krol **P:** aad krol
A: vivid | centre for design, studiomom | identity and design **M:** info@studiomom.nl

www.lounge72.com
D: kai heuser **C:** thorsten hayer **P:** kai heuser, thorsten hayer
A: lounge72 **M:** system@lounge72.com

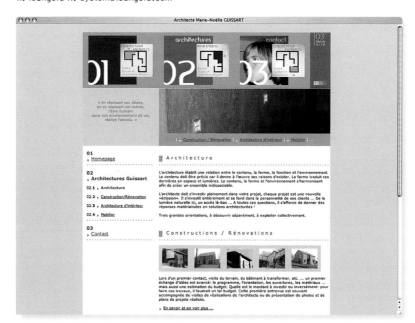

www.guissart.be/01/homepage.php
D: stéphane ghidetti
A: ghidetti.net **M:** stephane@ghidetti.net

www.netzfunk.org/?usr=d
D: david boardman
M: d-@netzfunk.org

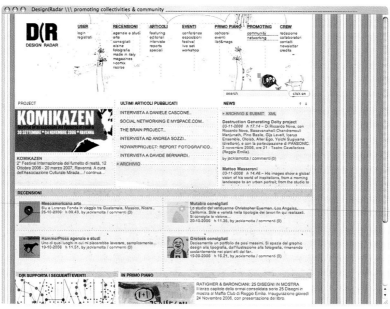

www.designradar.it
D: jacklamotta, mimmo manes, irene roggero C: christian mele, m. abuthiab
A: design(radar M: info@designradar.it

tool.com.mk
D: aleksandar kolov C: aleksandar kolov P: aleksandar kolov
A: xtool design M: aleksandar@digitalmedia.org.mk

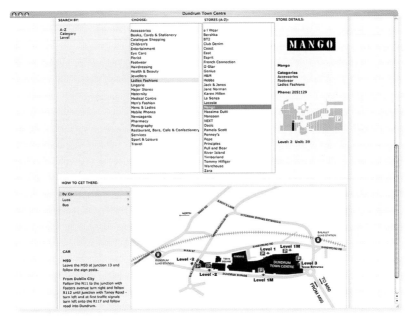

www.dundrum.ie
D: david jackson C: mick veale P: smudge design
A: smudge design M: www.smudgedesign.ie

www.sciencetools.net
D: maria garcia C: maria garcia P: elena pericas
A: science tools M: correo@sciencetools.net

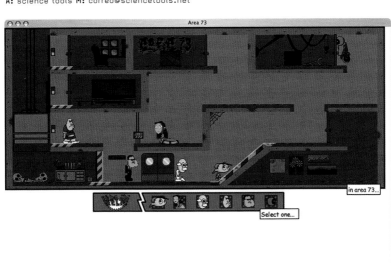

www.area73.pro.tc
D: 7unw3n C: 7unw3n P: 7unw3n
A: area-73 M: laujunwen@hotmail.com

locografix.com
D: jurgen van zachten C: joris hoogendoorn P: jurgen van zachten
A: locografix M: info@locografix.com

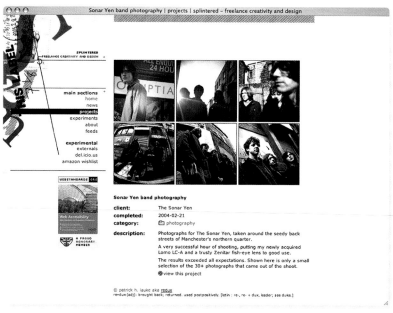

www.splintered.co.uk
D: patrick h. lauke C: patrick h. lauke P: patrick h. lauke
A: splintered M: redux@splintered.co.uk

www.thomasrusch.com
D: guido von scheider-marientreu, marc antosch C: g. von scheider-marientreu, k. abmeier
A: tilt design studio M: info@tiltdesignstudio.com

www.potipoti.com
D: nando cornejo, silvia salvador kopp C: nando cornejo P: nando cornejo, silvia s. kopp
A: potipoti graphic fashion M: post@nandocornejo.com, info@potipoti.com

www.tangolab.net
D: alejandro rumoino C: juan pablo espinoza P: esponoza, rumolino
A: j.p.e.free.fr, ar8.com.fr M: info@tangolab.net

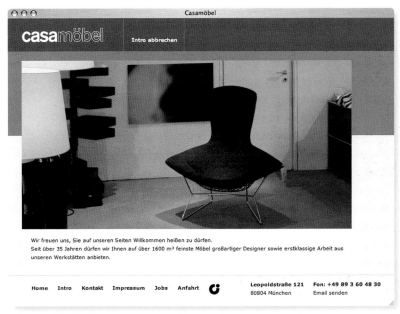

www.casamoebel.de
D: simon schories C: marco matthäus P: marco matthäus
A: pixelsinmotion M: marco@pixelsinmotion.de

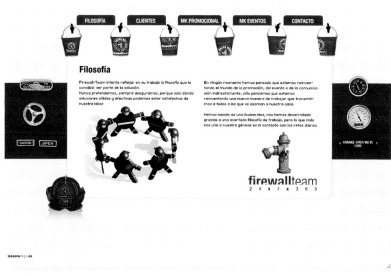

www.firewall-team.com
D: takeone dsgn C: takeone dsgn P: takeone dsgn
A: takeone dsgn conductas visuales s.l. M: tkl@takeone.es

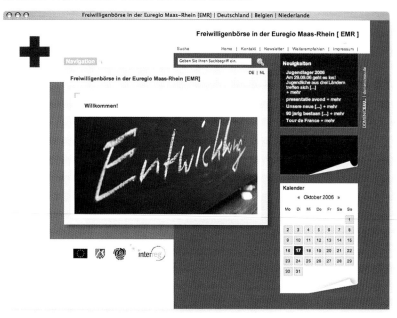

www.freiwilligenboerse-maas-rhein.eu
D: domeniceau | bdes. dominik welters P: rotes kreuz in der euregio maas-rhein
A: domeniceau | bdes. dominik welters M: www.domeniceau.de

www.anna-om-line.com
D: anna maría lópez lópez C: anna maría lópez lópez P: anna-om-line.com
A: anna-om-line.com M: hello@anna-om-line.com

www.alfaromeo.cl
D: juan paulo madriaza C: alvaro añón P: alfredo calderón
A: 4sale M: www.4sale.cl

www.sardinha-leite.pt
D: ricardo camarinha C: francisco leite castro
A: doismaisdois M: rcamarinha@doismaisdois.com

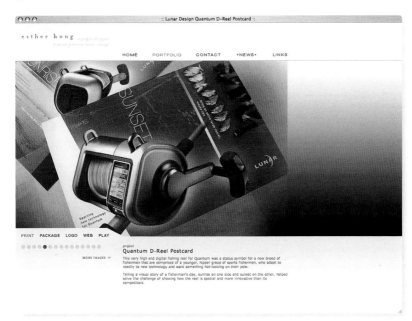

www.jinizm.com
D: esther hong
M: hong.esther@gmail.com

www.smallcarrot.com
D: gregor hofbauer C: sergiu baluta P: hana shimizu
A: small carrot llc M: info@smallcarrot.com

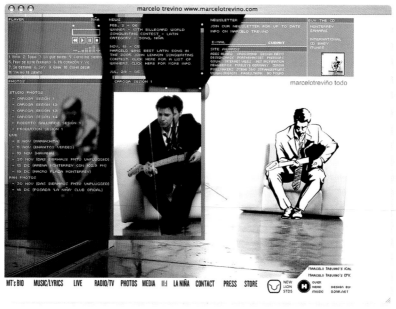

www.marcelotrevino.com
D: jenaro diaz, marcelo trevino C: jenaro diaz P: marcelo trevino, jenaro diaz
A: mt productions, djnr.net M: marcelo@marcelotrevino.com

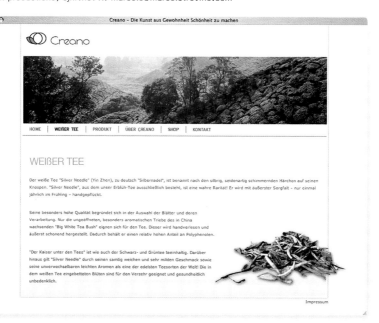

www.creano.com
D: guido eichhoff C: kai uebing P: creano
A: artboxx M: guido@artboxx.net

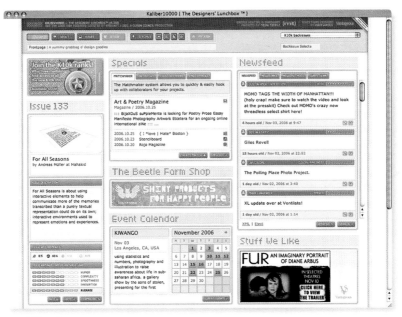

www.k10k.net
D: michael schmidt, toke nygaard C: michael schmidt, michael buzzard, per jørgensen
A: cuban council M: m@cubancouncil.com

www.hali.at
D: jürgen oberguggenberger C: milan figuric
A: kraftwerk / agentur für neue kommunikation gmbh M: feelgood@kraftwerk.co.at

www.treesquirrel.org
D: naz hamid C: naz hamid P: jen schuetz
A: weightshift M: jen@treesquirrel.org

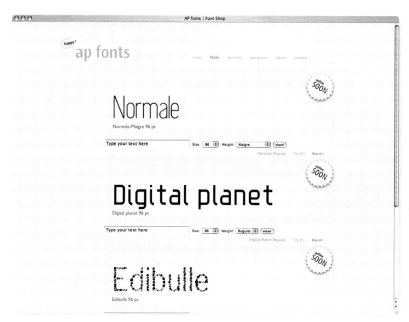

www.apfonts.com
D: thierry charbonnel, nicolas hoffmann, michel welfringer C: e. dupeux-maire, a. doury
A: autre planète, designers anonymes M: info@autreplanete.com

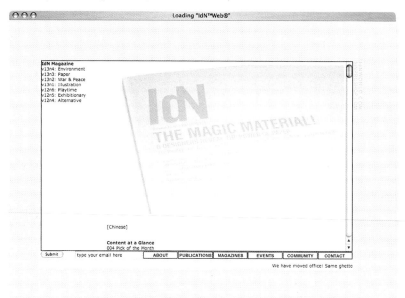

www.idnproshop.com/idnworld/index.htm
D: idn C: chris ng P: chris ng
A: idn M: info@idnworld.com

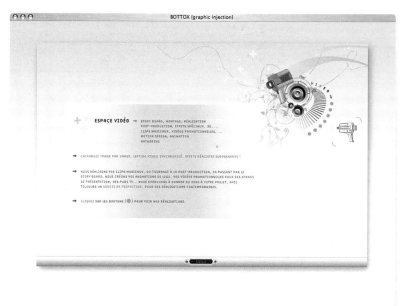

www.bottox.fr
D: c revest, n ouvrier, c spada, a pernaud P: bottox, v. landry, n henriot
A: bottox {graphic injection} M: contact@bottox.fr

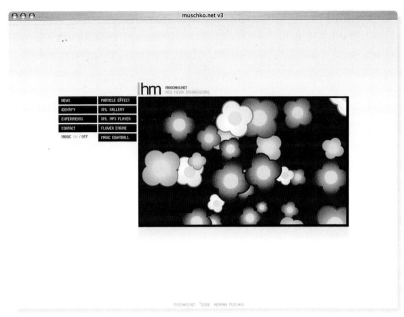

www.muschko.net
D: henning muschko
M: henning@muschko.net

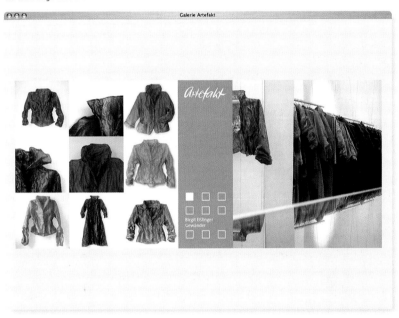

www.artefakt-muenchen.de
D: kathrin demand dickmann C: kathrin demand dickmann
A: blaupause M: mail@blaupause.com

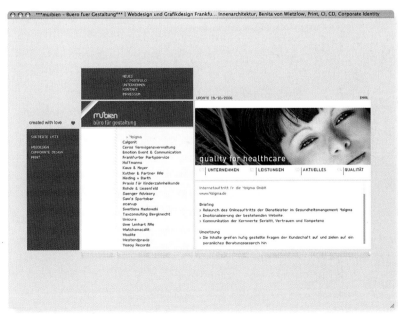

www.muibien.de
D: benita von wietzlow C: benita von wietzlow, romulo lazard
A: muibien // büro für gestaltung M: muibien@muibien.de

www.raulpina.net
D: raul pina
M: mail@raulpina.net

www.orangetape.com
D: david longworth P: andrew jalali
A: orange tape studios M: contact@orangetape.com

www.campingasolaze.com
D: rubén sánchez fernández
A: factoría norte M: ruben@factorianorte.com

44suburbia.org
D: melissa m
A: 44suburbia productions M: thegirl@44suburbia.org

www.outset.be
D: krasimir tsonev
M: web@outset.be

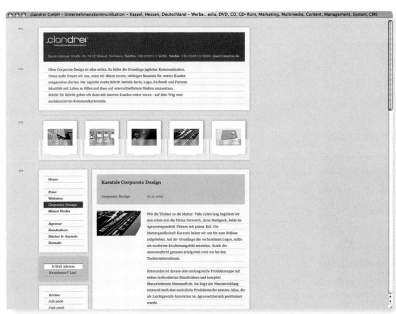

www.clandrei.de
D: kai brunning C: gilbert guttmann, robert schulke
A: clandrei gmbh M: clan@clandrei.de

www.bimaltailor.co.uk
D: bimal tailor
M: bimal.tailor@gmail.com

www.fdsmalaysia.com
D: eric lee C: eric lee P: eric lee
A: kqube interactive M: www.kqube.com

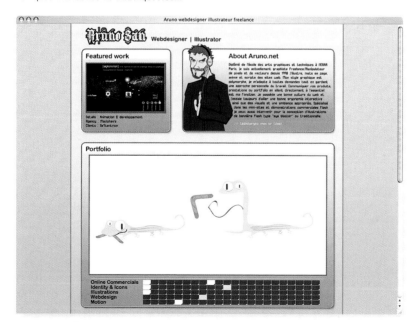

www.aruno.net
D: arno roddier C: arno roddier P: arno roddier
M: aruno@aruno.net

www.spyline.org
D: jan weiss
A: www.kreativkopf.tv M: j.weiss@kreativkopf.tv

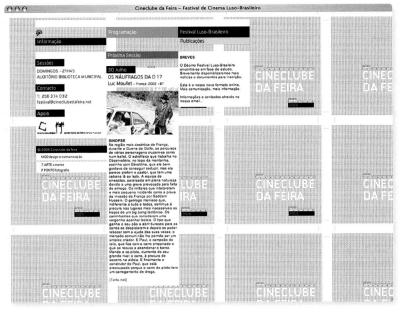

www.cineclubedafeira.net
D: susana queirós C: patricio macedo
A: moo design e comunicação M: www.moo.com.pt

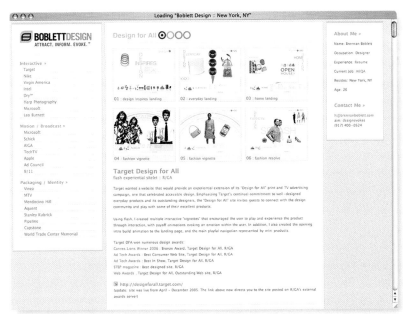

brennanboblett.com
D: brennan boblett
A: boblett design M: hi@brennanboblett.com

www.pushradio.com
D: damian garone, danny fania, oscar kayzak **C:** oscar kayzak, sherika **P:** damian garone
A: push radio **M:** info@pushradio.ca

www.pixelmedia.com
D: onur orhon **C:** ben alvord **P:** thomas obrey
A: pixelmedia, inc. **M:** tj@pixelmedia.com

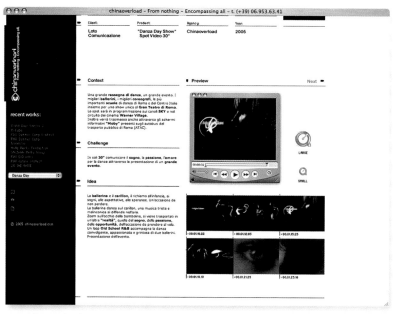

www.chinaoverload.com
D: christian surace zarzaca, alessandro simonini, umberto schiavella **C:** chinas
A: chinaoverload **M:** info@chinaoverload.com

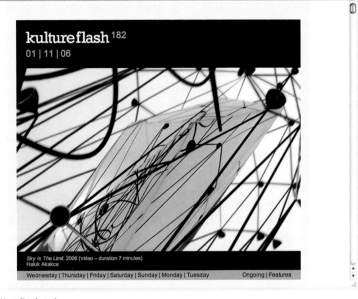

www.kultureflash.net
D: dixonbaxi P: julien dobbs-higginson
A: kultureflash ltd M: hq@kultureflash.net

www.kesovija-apartmani.com
D: goran grudic C: goran grudic P: goran grudic
A: gruda designs M: admin@kesovija-apartmani.com

www.alexxdesign.com
D: alex dodig
A: alexxdesign.com M: info.alexxdesign@gmail.com

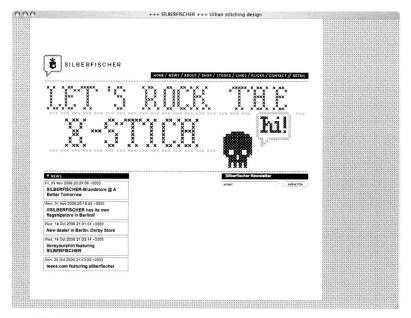

www.silberfischer.com
D: elke riethmüller C: elke riethmüller P: elke riethmüller, andré riethmüller
A: silberfischer M: mail@silberfischer.com

www.a-better-tomorrow.com
D: andré grünhoff C: till vollmer, michael hollauf P: andré grünhoff, tim lindemann
A: a better tomorrow M: info@a-better-tomorrow.com

www.szaboadam.hu
D: géza nyíry C: géza nyíry P: géza nyíry
A: nyk design M: info@nyk.hu

www.in-public.com
D: mathew wilson **C:** jenifer dunn **P:** erin staniland
A: with associates **M:** hello@withassociates.com

www.group94.com
D: pascal leroy **C:** group94 **P:** group94
A: group94 **M:** info@group94.com

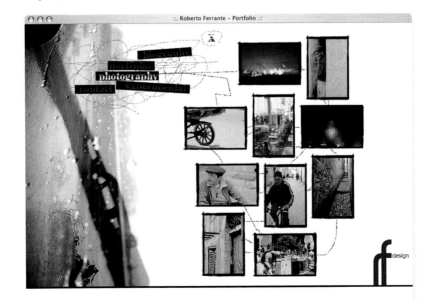

www.robertoferrante.net
D: roberto ferrante
M: info@robertoferrante.net

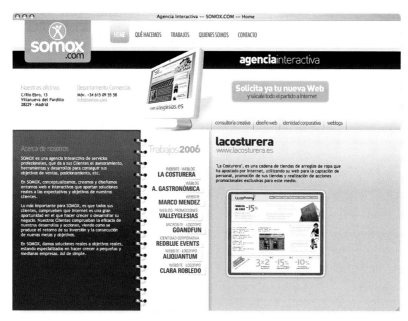

www.somox.com
D: óscar méndez C: francisco javier pastor P: jose antonio espinosa
A: somox.com M: info@somox.com

www.murava.com
D: michael clough C: paul k c cheung
A: compelite ltd M: www.compelite.net

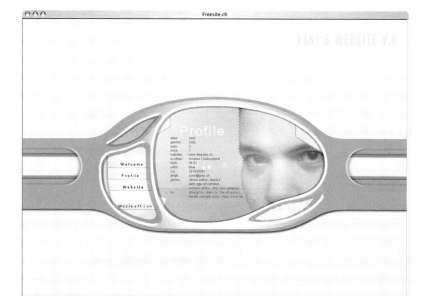

www.freesite.ch/v8
D: carli beeli
M: cbeeli@gmail.com

www.dasgelbehaus.ch
D: marc rinderknecht C: marc rinderknecht P: marc rinderknecht
A: kobebeef M: mr@kobebeef.ch

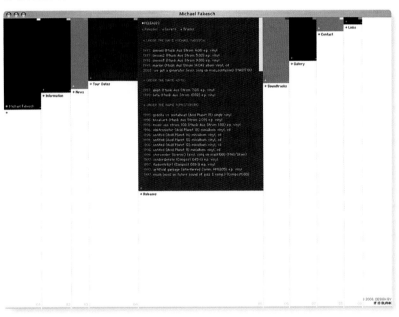

www.michaelfakesch.com
D: jurgis griskevicius C: it dironta, martynas niekelis P: it is blank
A: it is blank M: www.itisblank.com

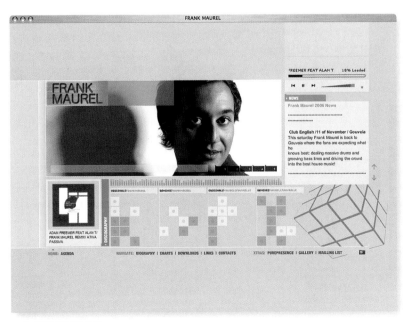

www.frankmaurel.com
D: diogo melo C: gustavo melo P: diogo melo
A: doismaisdois M: dmelo@doismaisdois.com

www.one-to-one-connection.com/index.shtml
D: radek vasicek C: richard minks P: otmar jursa
A: radekvasicek.com M: info@radekvasicek.com

www.crusoedesign.technographx.com
D: robinson chan C: robinson chan P: robinson chan
A: crusoe design M: crusoedesign@gmail.com

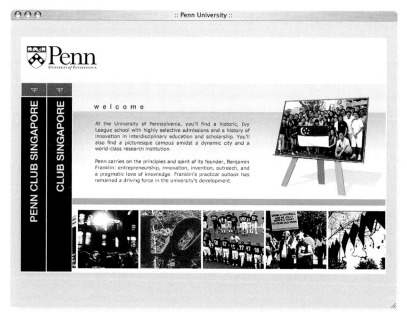

www.pennclub.sg
D: joanne ang C: terence teo P: joanne ang
A: caffeine media pte ltd M: www.caffeine.com.sg

www.simonwiffen.co.uk
D: simon wiffen
M: simon@simonwiffen.co.uk

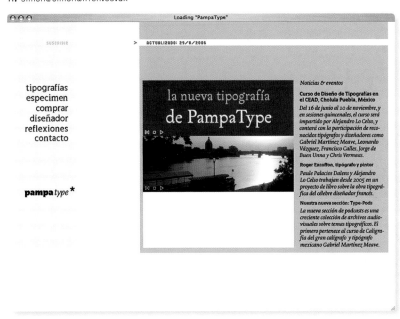

www.pampatype.com
D: alejandro lo celso C: isaias loaiza, maria de lourdes fuentes fuentes
A: pampatype digital foundry M: info@pampatype.com

www.e-wan.org
D: namwan chittchang
M: namwan@e-wan.org

www.eselboecksweinselektion.com
D: dian warsosumarto **C:** richard (hudi) hudeczek **P:** richard (hudi) hudeczek
A: jung von matt (vienna) **M:** www.mouse-media.net

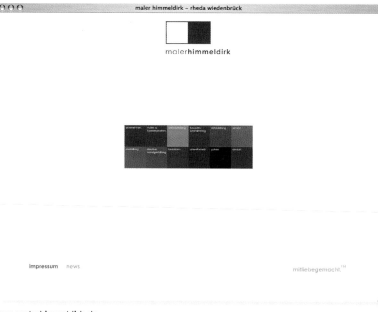

www.malerhimmeldirk.de
D: michaela duisberg, andre weier **C:** andre weier **P:** andre weier
A: nalindesign, zeichensprache **M:** info@nalindesign.com

www.suklaaterie.fi
D: fx. marciat **C:** fx. marciat **P:** fx. marciat
A: xy area **M:** www.xyarea.be

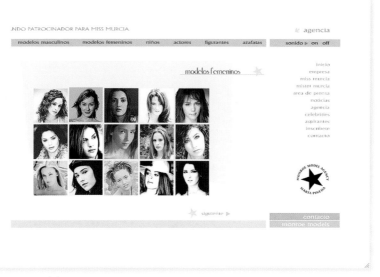

www.monroemodels.com
D: josé manuel maciá pérez C: josé manuel maciá pérez P: josé manuel maciá pérez
A: estudios pixel M: www.estudiospixel.com

www.uc48.net
D: tim harbour
A: uc48 design M: info@uc48.net

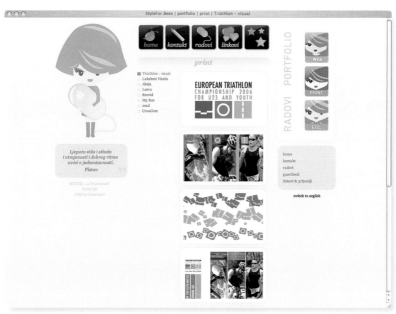

www.stylefor.biz
D: maja bencic C: davor peic
M: abeja@abeja.org

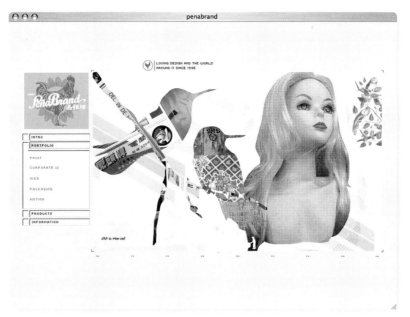

www.penabrand.com
D: luis pena C: luis pena, andreas tagger P: stacey olson woodruff
A: penabrand M: luis@penabrand.com

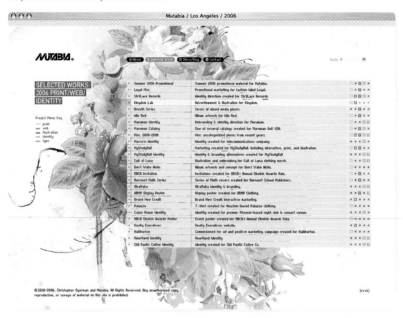

www.mutabia.com
D: christopher eyerman C: christopher eyerman
M: chris@mutabia.com

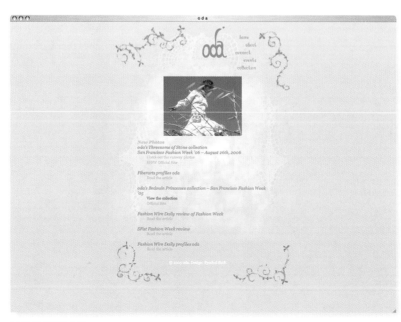

www.odastyle.com
D: bradley furnish C: bradley furnish P: symbol shift
A: symbol shift M: info@odastyle.com

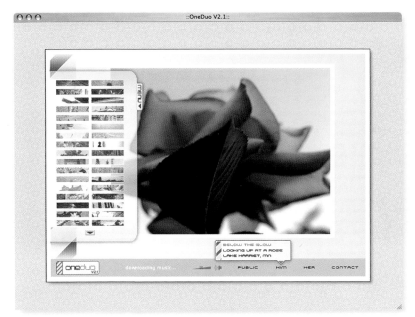

www.oneduo.net
D: tim beaufoy
A: pagecrush M: info@pagecrush.net

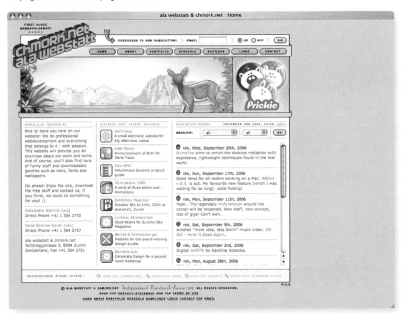

www.ala.ch
D: ala ramildi, rené etienne keller C: ala ramildi, rené etienne keller
A: ala webstatt, zürich M: inbox@ala.ch

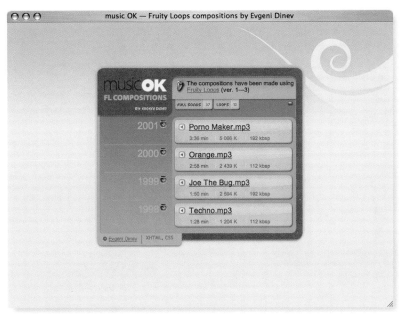

musicok.evgenidinev.com
D: evgeni dinev
M: contact@evgenidinev.com

www.cape-arcona.com
D: thomas schostok {ths}, stefan claudius C: thomas schostok {ths}
A: cape arcona type foundry M: general@cape-arcona.com

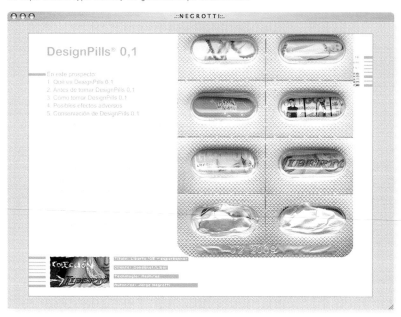

www.negrotti.com
D: jorge negrotti C: jorge negrotti P: jorge negrotti
A: design pills M: jorge@negrotti.com

www.sqcircle.com
D: danny burnside C: chris sees, george medve P: stella jordan
A: square circle media M: info@sqcircle.com

www.sandra-thomae.com
D: sasa huzjak C: sasa huzjak P: sasa huzjak, sandra thomae
A: plastikfantastik* M: sale@plastikfantastik.net

www.cabanadigital.com
D: jose cabana, patricia cabana C: jose cabana
A: cabana digital M: jose@cabanadigital.com

www.gangsterbosse.de
D: robert nippoldt
A: robert nippoldt | gestaltung und illustration M: robert@nippoldt.de

www.funbox.com.tw/babytoy/tomy/index.asp
D: liao mu wei P: liao mu wei
A: funbox studio M: wingerliao@pchome.com.tw

www.banz.tv
D: centrik isler C: centrik isler P: stefan banz
A: the webfactorY: cbc zurich M: www.banz.tv

www.splotches.org
D: johnschen kudos C: johnschen kudos P: johnschen kudos
A: splotches.org M: hello@johnkudos.com

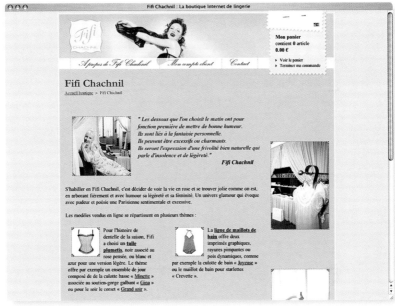

www.bouroullec.com
D: alain bellet C: alain bellet P: ronan bouroullec, erwan bouroullec
A: ronan bouroullec, erwan bouroullec M: info@bouroullec.com

www.boutique-fifichachnil.com
D: sokovision
M: eric.marillet@sokovision.com

www.meomi.com
D: meomi design
M: info@meomi.com

www.mandarine24.com
D: exo7.ca C: exo7.ca, sébastien touchette, frank lam, patrick matte P: mandarine 24
A: mandarine 24 M: info@mandarine24.com

www.illustranzana.it
D: illustranzana C: www.neogen.it P: chiara d´agostino
A: illustranzana M: chiara@illustranzana.it

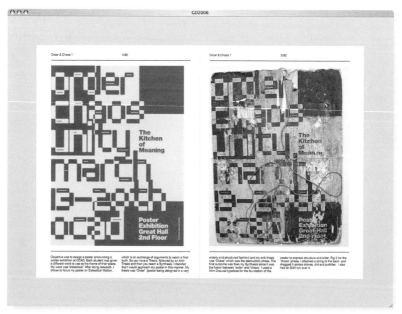

www.xrtions.com
D: gregory durrell
M: greg@xrtions.com

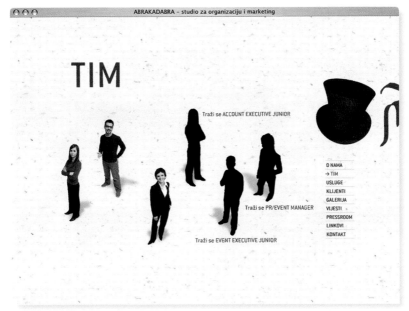

www.abrakadabra.hr
D: vladimir koncar C: gorjan agacevic
A: (r)evolution ltd. M: www.revolucija.hr

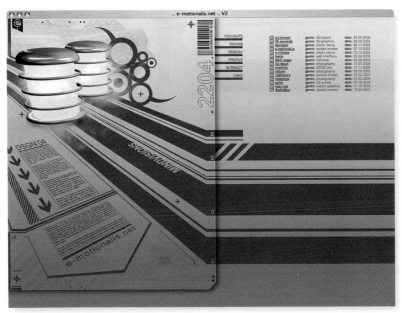

www.e-motionalis.net
D: axel achten
M: axel@subversion.be

www.dev4design.com
D: sébastien bonnet C: sébastien bonnet
A: dev4design M: seb@dev4design.com

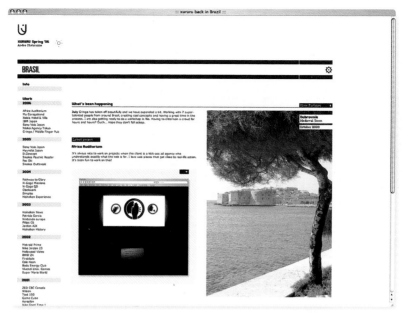

www.xururu.org
D: andre matarazzo C: andre matarazzo
M: andre.matarazzo@mac.com

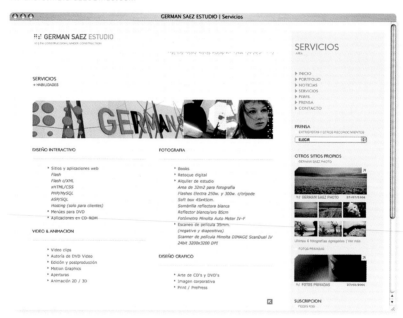

germansaez.com
D: germán saez
A: germán saez estudio M: germansaez.com

bigcartel.com
D: eric turner C: matt wigham P: indie labs
A: indie labs M: contact@indielabs.com

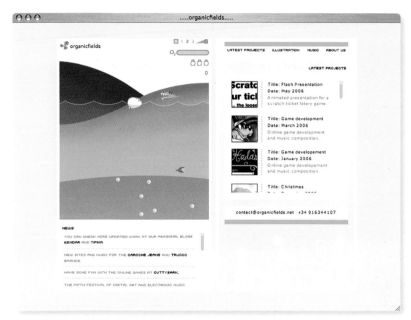

www.organicfields.net
D: patricia metola, mónica calvo C: carlos rincon P: organicfields
A: organicfields M: contact@organicfields.net

www.iprincipado.com
D: javier frades, rafael castillo C: f. estradera, s. gisbert P: principado inmobiliaria
A: grupo enfoca M: info@grupoenfoca.com

www.residenzabellifirenze.com
D: marco marini
A: webber M: marco.m@webberz.it

www.liquid.ag
D: ilja sallacz, sebastian onufszak C: s. onufszak P: ilja sallacz, carina orschulko
A: liquid | agentur für gestaltung M: onufszak@liquid.ag

www.arnhemspersagentschap.nl
D: boudewijn bakker
A: tripledesign M: www.tripledesign.nl

www.files-design.com
D: simon wang, kevin lee C: kevin lee, tai lin, yohji lin, tina ho P: kevin lee
A: files design group M: info@files-design.com

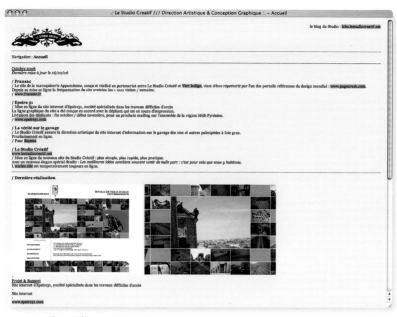

www.lestudiocreatif.net
D: thomas champion
A: le studio créatif M: thomas@lestudiocreatif.net

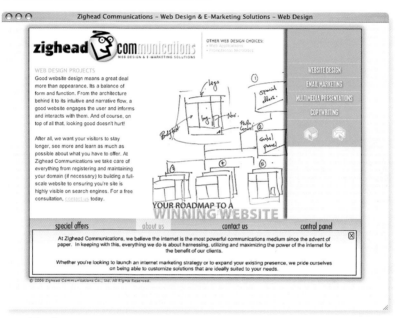

www.zighead.com
D: zahid ali C: zahid ali P: zahid ali
A: zighead communications M: zahid@zighead.com

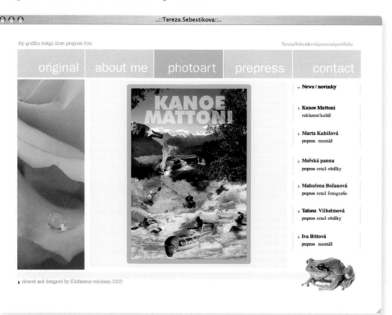

www.sebestikova.cz
D: mireque kodesh C: mireque kodesh
A: studio klubismus M: studio@klubismus.cz

www.bionerg.com.ar
D: santiago sadous C: santiago sadous P: santiago sadous
A: bionerg s.a. M: info@6elementos.com.ar

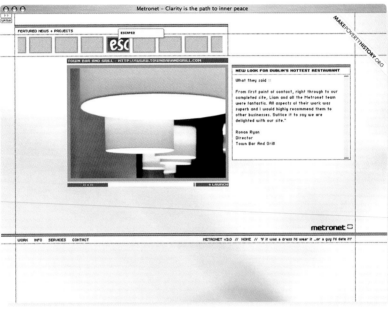

www.metronet.ie
D: liam chivers C: patrick o´reilly P: david healy
A: metronet limited M: info@metronet.ie

www.twosides.com.mk
D: aleksandar pesevski C: aleksandar pesevski P: aleksandar pesevski
A: mightycreation M: sasho_webmaster@yahoo.com

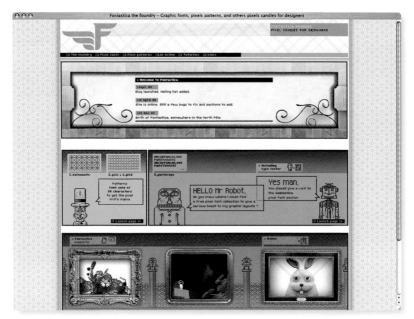

www.fontastica.com
D: antony squizzato
A: periscope creations M: anto@fontastica.com

www.compuart.com
D: stefan behringer C: juergen wunderle
A: d:\sign creativeconcepts M: contact@dsign.de

www.lesdoigtsdelhomme.com
D: joolz morel C: nat hayles P: sam hayles
A: dose-productions M: contact@dose-productions.com

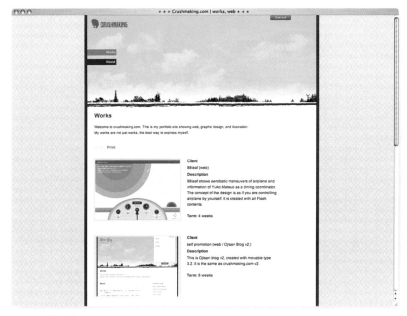

www.crushmaking.com
D: yu matsumoto
A: crushmaking M: mail@crushmaking.com

www.gemstoneprojecten.nl
D: remco van der toorn C: remco van der toorn
A: studio plankton M: info@studioplankton.nl

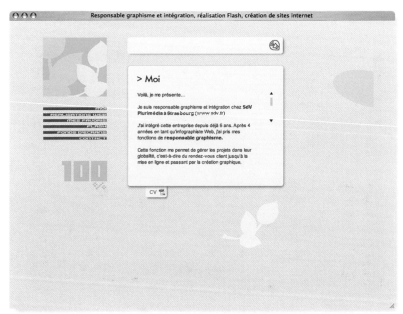

www.onlinegraph.com
D: gury fabrice C: gury fabrice P: onlinegraph
A: personal project M: guryf@wanadoo.fr

186

www.thenest.nu
D: jenny karlsson
M: jenny@thenest.nu

www.newmediadesign.pt
D: new media design
M: info@newmediadesign.pt

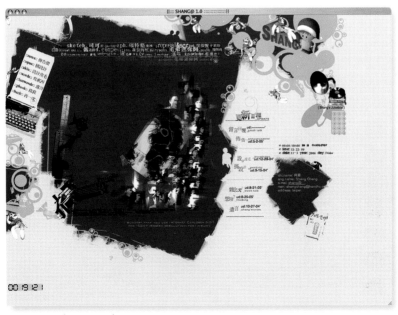

shang.idv.tw/shang2004/index.html
D: shang chang
M: shang.sergio@gmail.com

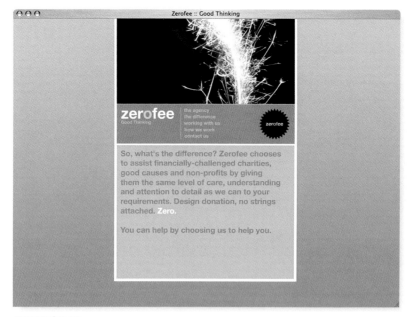

www.zerofee.org
D: paul buck, ela kosmaczewska C: paul buck P: paul buck
A: zerofee M: info@zerofee.org

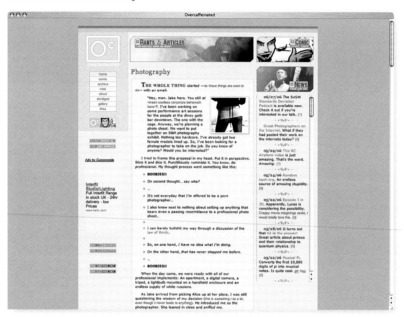

www.overcaffeinated.net
D: sergio villarreal
M: sergio@overcaffeinated.net

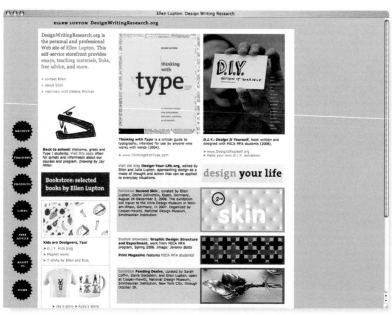

www.designwritingresearch.org
D: ellen lupton
M: elupton@designwritingresearch.org

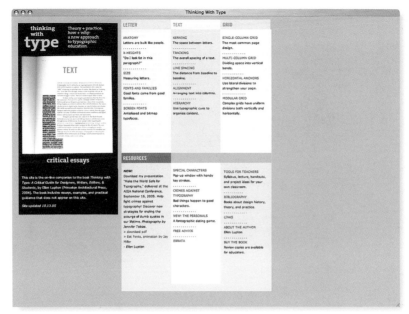

www.thinkingwithtype.com
D: ellen lupton C: ellen lupton P: princeton architectural press
A: ellen lupton M: elupton@designwritingresearch.org

www.creaktif.com
D: jocker C: mopi
A: creaktif M: team@creaktif.com

www.cresk.nl
D: gert van duinen
A: cresk design M: design@cresk.nl

www.daninko.ca
D: dan nanasi
A: daninko M: dan@daninko.ca

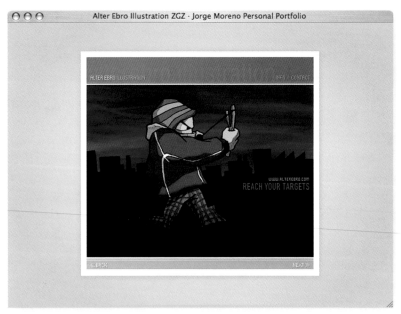

www.alterebro.com
D: jorge moreno
A: alter ebro M: info@alterebro.com

www.juggernart.com/index2.html
D: markus eichler C: markus eichler
A: juggernart.com M: juggernart@juggernart.com

xsthestore.com
D: luis aparicio, ciro urdaneta C: rodolfo sauce, c. urdaneta, l. giraldez
A: image & web solution M: curdaneta@iws.com.ve

www.tolugenova.com
D: artiva design P: daniele de batté, davide sossi
A: artiva design M: www.artiva.it

www.anovadesign.com
D: jesper bentzen C: jesper bentzen P: jesper bentzen
A: anova | jesper bentzen M: jbentzen@anovadesign.com

www.volumeone.com
D: matt owens
A: volumeone llc M: info@volumeone.com

www.designchapel.com
D: robert lindstrom
A: designchapel M: info@designchapel.com

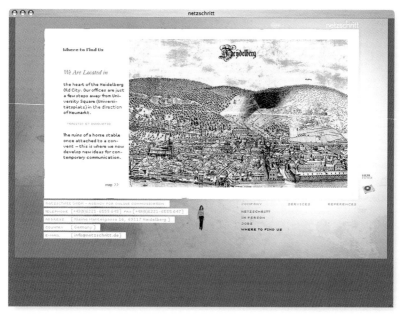

www.netzschritt.de
D: marc zach C: alexander mechler P: netzschritt gmbh
A: netzschritt gmbh M: info@netzschritt.de

www.progressmedia.net/welcome.htm
D: davide g. aquini
A: whynet.info M: davide@whynet.info

www.zueei.com
D: karen yeung C: simon swain, obscure P: karen yeung
M: karen@zueei.com

www.once-upon-a-forest.com
D: maruto
M: www.once-upon-a-forest.com

Welcome, oh weary Internet traveler. You've arrived at the web site of Sandstrom Design. Well 'whoop-de-doo,' you're probably saying, 'another self-impressed, preciously-perfect ode to Helvetica Bold and Tidy Bowl packaging.' Hardly. In keeping with our philosophy of mixing the creation of stunning design work with a smattering of adolescent humor, we've built a digital home that has many nontraditional rooms to explore. See how you can turn a busy and productive afternoon into a complete wasted effort by squandering your time away with the Client/Project Match Game or Stupid Design Trick. Find out if together we'll be like Paul Newman and Joanne Woodward or more like Tonya Harding and Jeff Gillooly by taking our scientifically-designed *Client Compatibility Test* . Find out who we work for and how the hell we stay in business. So **enter**, explore and if the spirit should move you, hire us to do your next corporate identity, package design, in-store promotion, trade show booth, brochure, letterhead, ad, direct mail piece, signage, film titles or poster. Just don't send us any nasty e-mails.

www.sandstromdesign.com
D: steve sandstrom, jon olsen, s. morrow, m. cozza C: j. bohls, c. papasadero P: k. bohls
A: sandstrom design M: rick@sandstromdesign.com

www.anne-sophie-mutter.com
D: stephan schmidt C: peter morgner, florentin hauber, a. stürz P: a. p. mutter, s. schmidt
A: farbe8.com, a.p.mutter kommunikation M: info@farbe8.com

www.imagemakerfm.net/mmps/index.htm
D: regionable
M: regionable@yahoo.com

hort.kiev.ua
D: sergey kononenko C: sergey kononenko P: hort
M: grafika.com.ua

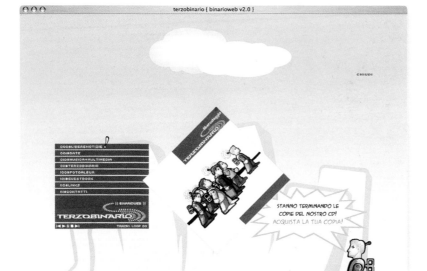

www.terzobinario.it
D: carlo zapponi C: carlo zapponi P: carlo zapponi
A: digitalfog M: webdesign@digitalfog.it

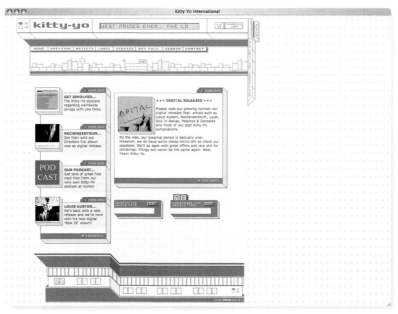

www.kitty-yo.de
D: gosub communications, peter prautzsch C: gosub communications
A: kitty-yo musicproductions, berlin M: office@kitty-yo.com

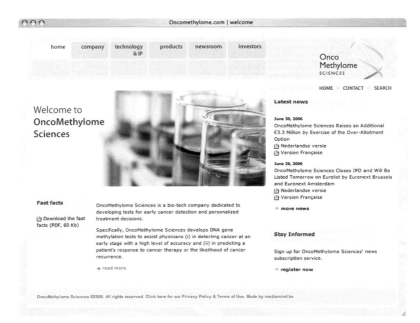

www.oncomethylome.com
D: ram broekaert
A: mediamind.be **M:** ram@mediamind.be

www.dumon.es
D: román rodríguez **C:** miquel lópez
A: mires estudi de comunicació **M:** www.miresweb.com

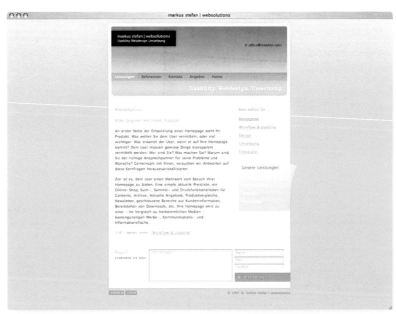

www.mstefan.com
D: markus stefan **C:** markus stefan
A: markus stefan | websolutions **M:** office@mstefan.com

www.splittheatom.com
D: darren bull, craig orchard C: dave ferguson P: anthony smith
A: split the atom ltd M: info@splittheatom.com

www.starcostruzioni.it
D: giovanni frassi C: giovanni frassi P: giovanni frassi
A: ovosodo web & publishing M: info@ovosodo.net

www.slangbcn.com
D: squizzo
M: info@squizzo.com

www.400.co.uk
D: sam willard C: sam willard P: sam willard
A: 400 communications ltd M: design@400.co.uk

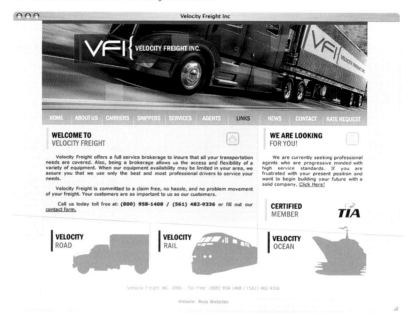

www.velocityfreight.com
D: leonardo rafael schneider C: leonardo rafael schneider P: bruce r. seidenstein
A: aventura websites M: bruce@aventurawebsites.com

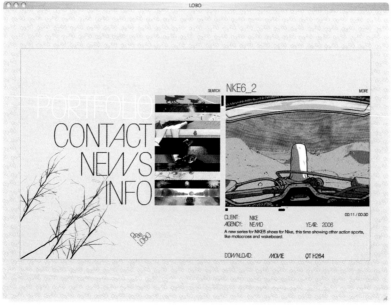

www.lobo.cx
D: carlos bíla P: 14 bits
A: www.14bits.com.br M: info@lobo.cx

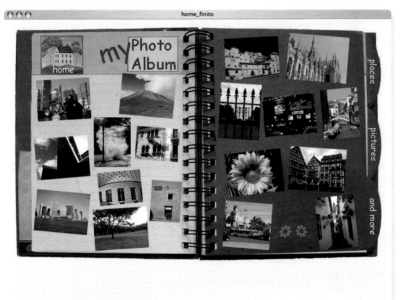

www.dexim.it
D: alchimedia srl C: massimiliano mureddu P: alchimedia srl
A: alchimedia srl M: cmolinari@alchimedia.com

www.webgarda.com/sito_photo_album/pagine/home_finito.html
D: alessandra zermini
M: troppotitti@yahoo.com

www.induplus.eu
D: kristof van rentergem C: kristof van rentergem P: kristof van rentergem
A: weblounge M: www.weblounge.be

www.c06studio.com
D: chi chau lam C: chi chau lam P: chi chau lam
A: c06 studio M: info@c06studio.com

www.edmerritt.com
D: ed merritt
A: ed merritt studios M: ed@edmerritt.com

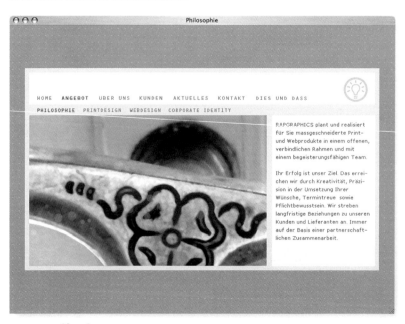

www.rapgraphics.ch
D: patricia mengis, ariane fankhauser, g. lutz C: a. fankhauser P: mengis, fankhauser
A: rapgraphics M: contact@rapgraphics.ch

www.quadrar.com
D: filipe cavaco, alexandre r. gomes C: alexandre r. gomes
A: bürocratik M: alex@burocratik.com

www.arnaldoroman.net
D: a roman, lilliam nieves C: daniel arnaldo roman P: grupo probeta studios
A: grupo probeta studios M: info@grupoprobeta studios

www.cafeazul.com.br
D: raphael simas C: leandro guedes P: igor simas
A: café azul mídia digital M: igor@cafeazul.com.br

www.nublue.co.uk
D: michael ashworth C: thomas ashworth P: nufuture ltd
A: nublue M: michael@nublue.co.uk

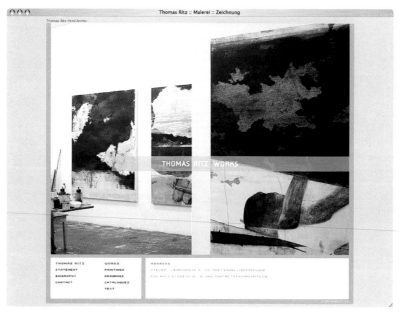

www.thomas-ritz.ch
D: thomas ritz C: thomas ritz P: thomas ritz
A: ritz & häfliger visuelle gestaltung M: t.ritz@ritz-haefliger.ch

www.anabelamor.be/hola
D: anabel amor C: tom cremelie P: mentor kortjik
A: anabel amor M: anabel@anabelamor.be

www.breathewords.com
D: adriana de barros C: adriana de barros P: adriana de barros
A: breathewords.com M: www.breathewords.com

www.rivena.com
D: alpaslan deveci, erkan deveci C: alpaslan deveci P: alpaslan deveci
A: rivena M: info@rivena.com

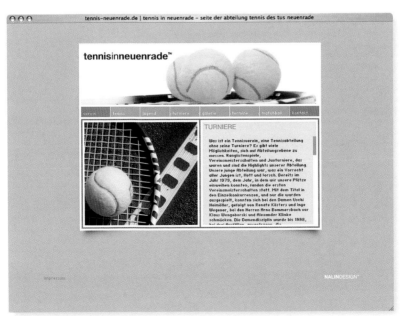

www.tennis-neuenrade.de
D: andre weier C: andre weier P: andre weier
A: nalindesign M: info@nalindesign.com

www.oneduasan.com/pixel
D: mervin ng man meng
A: manmeng M: siaukia@gmail.com

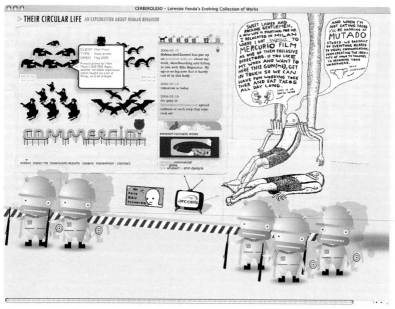

www.cerberoleso.it
D: lorenzo fonda C: alessandro d´andrea
M: cembro@cerberoleso.it

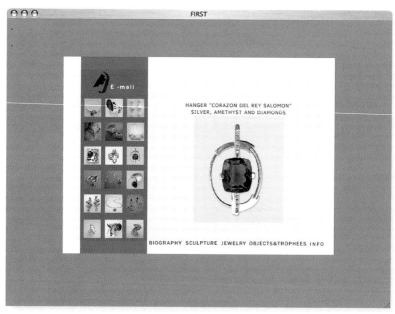

www.lianekatsuki.com
D: carmen t. barros C: carmen t.barros
A: puntobarros M: contact@puntobarros.com

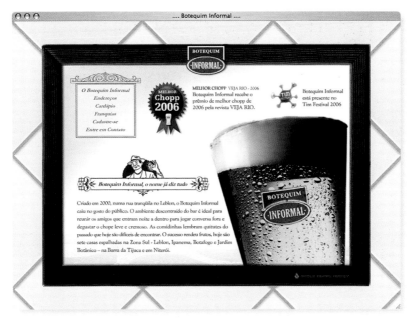

www.botequiminformal.com.br
D: bruno chamma C: rodrigo albuquerque P: bruno magalhães
A: kindle digital agency M: www.kindle.com.br

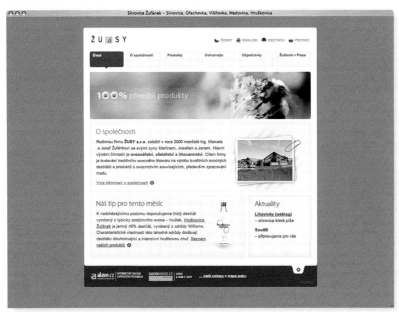

www.zufanek.cz
D: vit dlouhy C: vit dlouhy P: martin zufanek
A: zusy s.r.o. M: martin@zufanek.cz

www.insightmedianetworks.com
D: santiago sadous C: santiago sadous P: 6elementos_creative.solutions
A: insight media networks international M: info@6elementos.com.ar

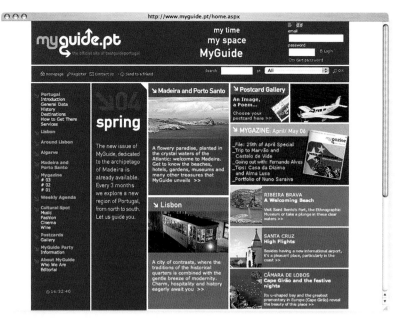

www.myguide.pt
D: transglobal
A: transglobal, comunicação e publicidade M: info@transglobalsite.com

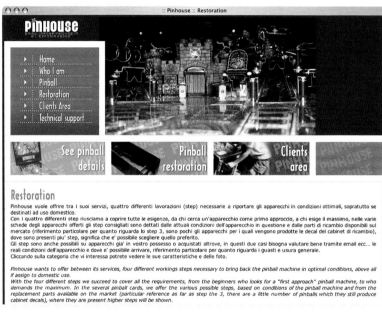

www.pinhouse.it
D: arianna boz C: arianna boz P: arianna boz
A: virtual edge M: www.virtualedge.it

www.usemedia.com
D: joes koppers C: joes koppers P: joes koppers
A: use M: use@usemedia.com

www.designammain.de
D: christian kunz C: christian kunz P: kolossaldigital
A: kolossaldigital M: designammain.de

www.abrilmobiliario.com
D: edigma.com
M: info@abrilmobiliario.com

www.dominicwilcox.com
D: dominic wilcox
M: info@dominicwilcox.com

www.micksmedia.com
D: mick veale C: mick veale P: mick veale
A: micksmedia M: www.micksmedia.com

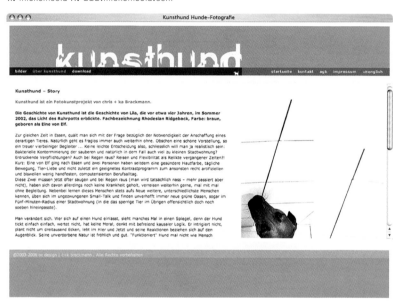

www.kunsthund.de
D: chris brackmann, ka brackmann C: ka brackmann P: oz-lab
A: oz M: www.oz-zone.de

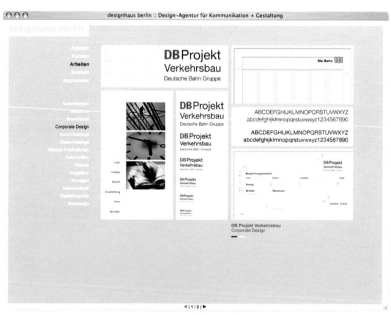

www.designhaus-berlin.de
D: manuel radde C: felix wittig P: bernd krause
A: designhaus berlin M: office@designhaus-berlin.de

louiemantia.com

D: louie mantia C: patrick yan P: louie mantia
A: louie mantia M: louiemantia.com

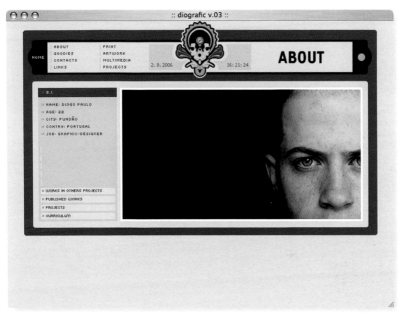

www.diografic.com

D: diogo paulo C: diogo paulo P: diogo paulo
A: ruadesign M: mail@diografic.com

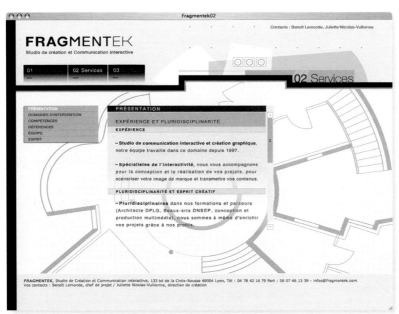

www.fragmentek.com

D: juliette nicolas-vullierme C: benoît lemonde P: fragmentek
A: fragmentek M: jnvullierme@fragmentek.com

www.nathan-baume.com
D: frederik vanderfaeillie C: gaëtan lafaut P: nathan-baume maroquinier
A: chilli design & multimedia M: info@chilli.be

www.hildundk.de
D: andreas kretzer C: andreas kretzer P: andreas kretzer
A: kretzer - architektur und szenenbild M: kontakt@architekturetc.de

www.estudiodepublicidad.com
D: josé ángel barrera C: magalí piterman
A: arrontes y barrera, estudio de publicidad M: arrontesybarrera@estudiodepublicidad.com

www.jonathanyuen.com
D: jonathan yuen
M: info@jonathanyuen.com

www.sepia-agentur.ch
D: reto portmann, daniela schmid C: sascha bachmann, stefan egli P: sepia
A: sepia M: info@sepia-agentur.ch

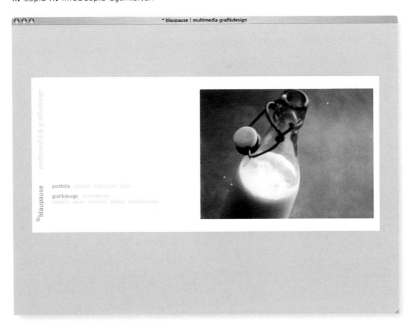

www.kathrindemand.de
D: kathrin demand dickmann C: kathrin demand dickmann P: kathrin demand dickmann
A: blaupause M: mail@blaupause.com

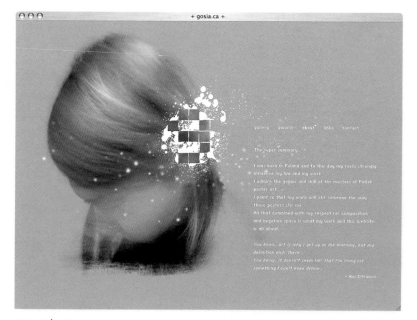

www.gosia.ca
D: gosia, piotrek C: piotrek.ca P: gosia, piotrek
A: gosia M: gosia@gosia.ca

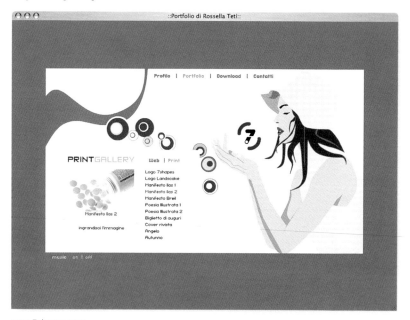

www.7shapes.com
D: rossella teti
M: r.teti@alice.it

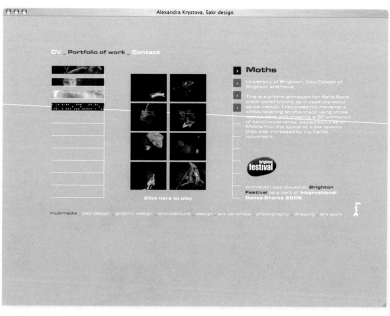

www.sakr-design.com
D: alexandra krystova
A: sakr design M: sakr@email.cz

www.jasonsiu.com
D: david yu
A: dhky M: sifu@dhky.com

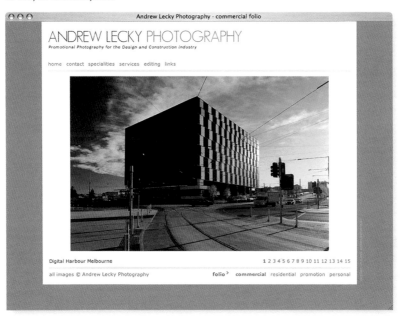

www.leckyphoto.com.au
D: karl hedner C: karl hedner P: jesper hedner
A: julian kommunikation M: info@julian.se

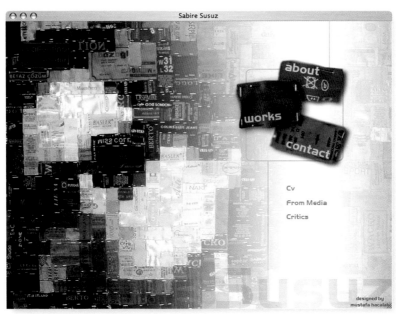

www.sabiresusuz.com
D: mustafa hacalaki C: mustafa hacalaki P: sabire susuz
M: hacalaki@yahoo.com

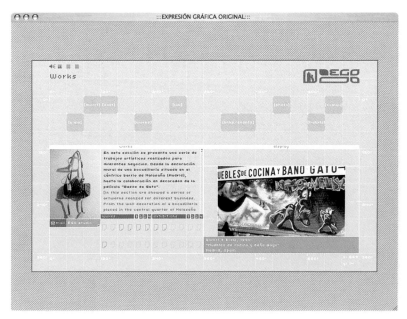

www.egocrew.com
D: jorge negrotti C: jorge negrotti P: jorge negrotti
A: design pills M: jorge@negrotti.com

home.kimo.com.tw/0922407314/index01.html
D: yu-chi chen
A: erosdesign M: yochichen@hotmail.com

www.djmarcoscruz.com
D: gamonoso C: madden P: gamonoso
A: gamonoso*graphics M: www.gamonoso.com

www.mariorivera.it
D: giovanni roncoroni C: giovanni roncoroni P: giovanni roncoroni
A: groncoueb M: gronco.ac@tin.it

www.microbians.com
D: gabriel suchowolski
A: the cocoe conspiracy M: microbians.bulk@gmail.com

www.koingosw.com
D: josh hague C: josh hague P: josh hague
A: koingo software M: main@koingosw.com

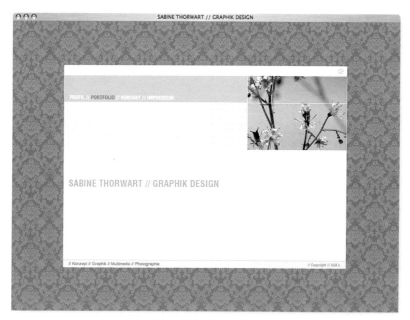

www.freshsign.de
D: sabine thorwart C: sabine thorwart
A: designtouch M: info@freshsign.de

www.photomagazine.it
D: stefano arcidiacono
A: photorevolt.com M: info@photomagazine.it

www.windcitymoon.com.tw
D: denis lin, whylan yeh C: borway lin P: denis lin
A: www.eyewasabi.com M: denis0516@gmail.com

www.hel-looks.com
D: sampo karjalainen P: liisa jokinen
M: info@hel-looks.com

www.flashlightdesign.com
D: peter flaschner
M: info@flashlightdesign.com

www.adibas.nl
D: bas boerman C: bas boerman P: bas boerman
A: adibas M: info@adibas.nl

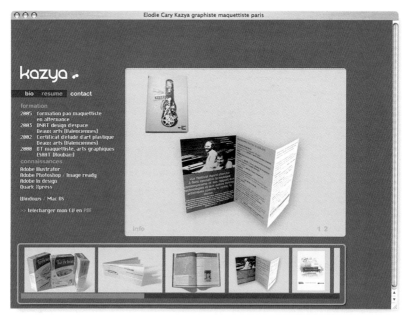

www.kazya.net
D: arno roddier, elodie cary P: elodie cary
A: aruno M: elodie@kazya.net

www.vak18.com
D: t. muusers C: t. muusers, p.a.h. meeuwsen P: t. muusers
A: vak18 M: info@vak18.com

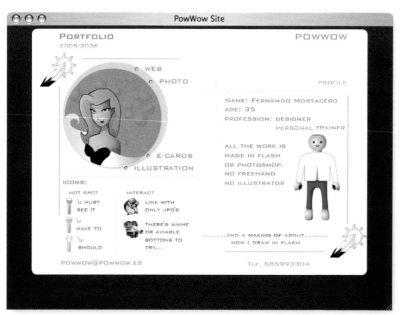

www.powwow.es
D: fernando mostacero serra
M: powwow@powwow.es

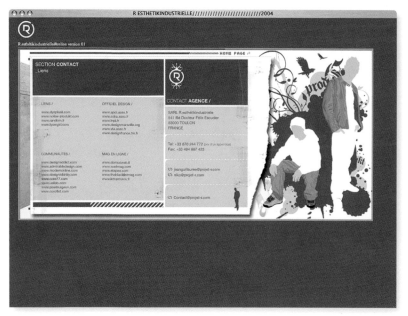

www.projet-r.com
D: jean guillaume leprieur C: nicolas cocheteux
A: r.esthetikindustrielle M: contact@projet-r.com

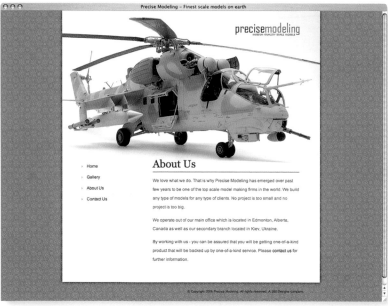

precisemodeling.com
D: 350 designs
M: info@350designs.com

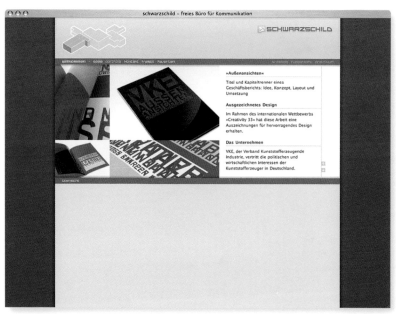

www.schwarzschild.de
D: stefan frey, karsten müller C: karsten müller
A: schwarzschild - freies büro für kommunikation M: kontakt@schwarzschild.de

www.advicegaleria.it
D: nepi livio, valbusa stefano, franceschi gianni C: albertini riccardo P: galeria
A: galeria advice M: info@advicegaleria.it

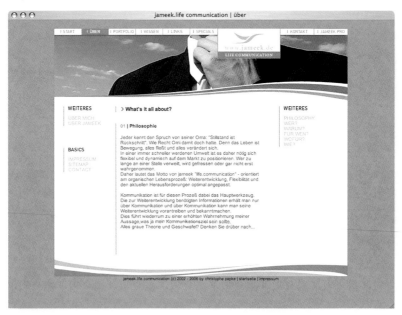

www.jameek.de/index2.html
D: christophe papke C: christophe papke P: christophe papke
A: jameek M: christophe@jameek.de

www.icondrawer.com
D: eugen buzuk
A: icondrawer M: buz@icondrawer.com

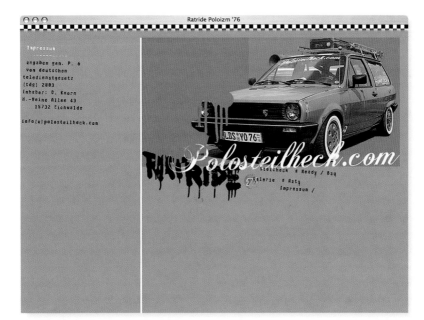

www.polosteilheck.com
D: daniel knorn C: daniel knorn P: daniel knorn
A: kombinat-ost M: info@polosteilheck.com

www.grenouilleonline.be
D: bart venken
M: bart.venken@chello.be

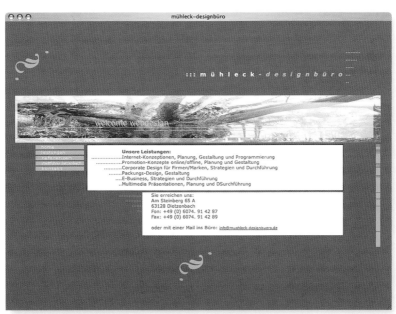

www.muehleck-designbuero.de
D: friederike mühleck C: friederike mühleck P: friederike mühleck
A: muehleck-designbuero M: info@muehleck-designbuero.de

www.salted.com
D: paul farnell C: paul farnell P: paul farnell
A: salted M: paul@salted.com

www.damiengilles.com
D: damien gilles
M: contact@damiengilles.com

www.stefine.com
D: charles C: david P: david
A: the stefine M: www.thestefine.com

www.rasterized.org
D: luis carlos araujo C: chris bauman P: luis carlos araujo, keith kennedy
A: creativestem.com M: luis@rasterized.org

www.amedion.de
D: alexander wilms C: alexander wilms P: alexander wilms
A: amedion M: info@amedion.de

www.lisad.com
D: alois gstöttner, blois.at C: alois gstöttner, blois.at
A: lisa d fashion berlin M: in@lisad.com

www.pavlikmicek.com
D: pavel micek
M: www.pavlikmicek.com

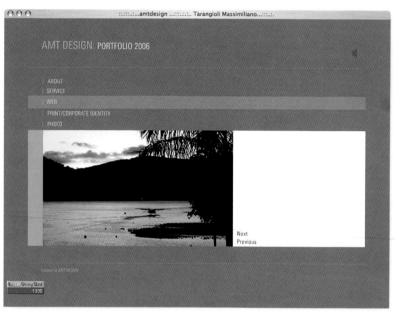

www.amtdesign.it
D: tarangioli massimiliano
A: amtdesign M: contact@amtdesign.it

www.designiq.eu
D: filip blazek, radek sidun C: vizus P: filip blazek
A: designiq, prague M: studio@designiq.cz

www.bleep.com
D: matt pyke C: chris mcgrail, dan london P: warp records
A: bleep M: info@bleep.com

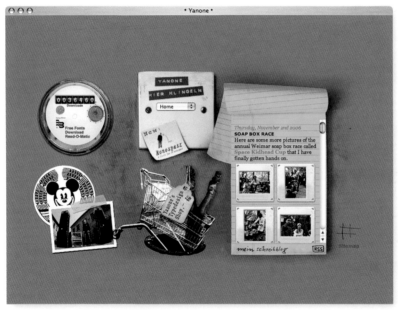

www.yanone.de
D: yanone
M: post@yanone.de

www.faile.net
D: faile C: renda morton P: faile
M: info@faile.net

www.typofonderie.com
D: jean françois porchez C: jean francois porchez, jérôme vogel
A: porchez typofonderie M: info@typofonderie.com

www.booreiland.nl
D: menno huisman, wimer hazenberg C: wimer hazenberg P: andré weenink
A: booreiland M: info@booreiland.nl

www.yoriwa.com
D: beto espitia, charity read C: michael switzer P: j. barone, r. balmaseda, k. carbonnet
A: solutionset for yoriwa, inc. M: karen@yoriwa.com

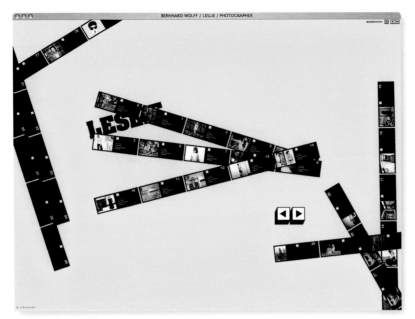

www.bernhardwolff.com
D: michael franken C: michael franken
A: bernhard wolff M: leslie@edsfirearms.com,

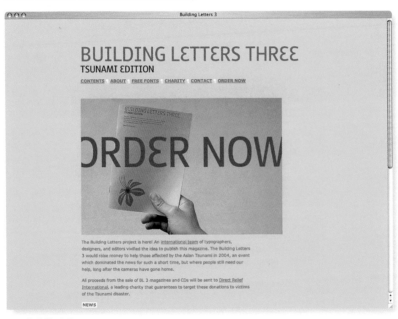

www.buildingletters.org
D: filip blazek
A: designiq, prague M: studio@designiq.cz

www.capacity.tv
D: ellerey gave C: benji thiem, raquel galan, jennifer gave P: jill marklin
A: capacity M: info@capacity.tv

www.proefjes.nl
D: tijn snoodijk C: arno verweij
A: stichting proefjes M: info@proefjes.nl

www.nothing.ch
D: bastiaan van rooden C: urban etter P: bastiaan van rooden
A: nothing from outer space M: spot@nothing.ch

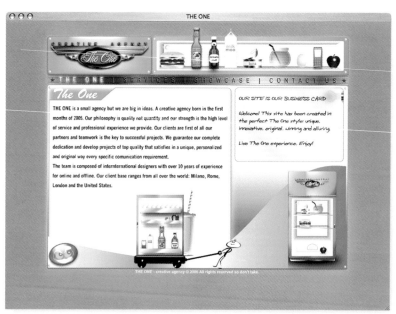

www.the-one.it
D: stefano sales C: fabrizio danieli P: stefano sales
A: the one M: sasales@the-one.it

www.mediaweb.pt
D: joão prior C: nelson rodrigues P: joão prior
A: mediaweb creations M: geral@mediaweb.pt

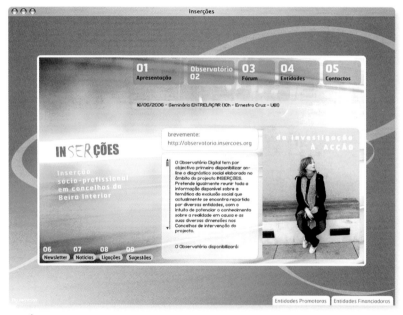

www.insercoes.org
D: paulo afonso C: paulo afonso P: ubi_ces
A: semmais & ubi_ces M: www.semmais.com

www.villakakelbont-zwolle.nl
D: niels van der velden C: niels van der velden P: niels van der velden
A: dare2dream M: niels@dare2dream.nl

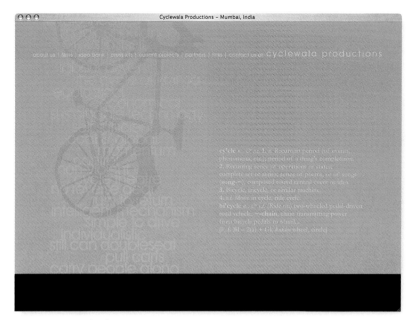

www.cyclewalaproductions.com
D: anand gandhi C: anand gandhi P: cyclewala productions
A: cyclewala productions M: www.cyclewalaproductions.com

www.417north.com
D: greg huntoon
M: www.gofarm.la

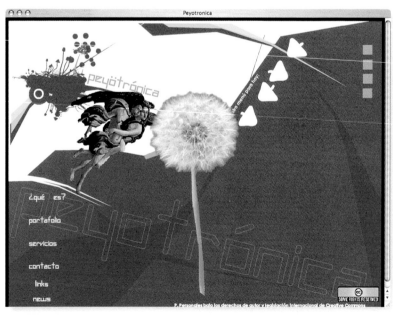

www.peyotronica.com
D: laura montanaro, rené serrano C: peyotronica diseño estudio
M: info@peyotronica.com

www.foroarq.com
D: gabriel beas C: gabriel beas P: gabriel beas
A: mtgp_design M: gabriel@foroarq.com

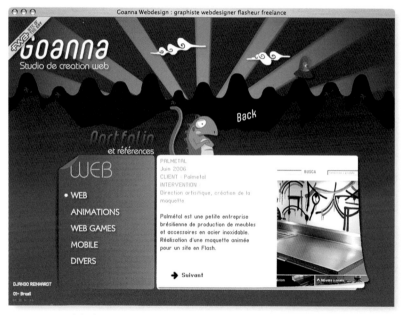

www.goanna-webdesign.com
D: goanna
A: studio goanna webdesign M: goanna-webdesign@hotmail.fr

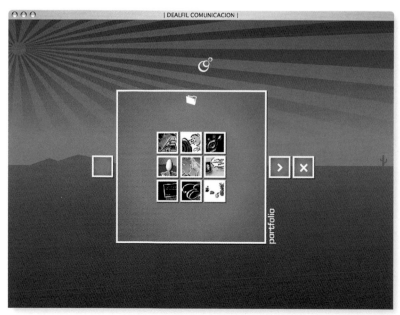

www.dealfil.com
D: alberto álvarez C: daniel sánchez P: dealfil estudio
A: dealfil estudio M: alberto@dealfil.com

www.carmenardura.com
D: rubén martínez C: rubén martínez P: rubén martínez
A: puré M: www.puregrafico.com

www.extremehairsaloon.com
D: yeva chow C: yeva chow P: yeva chow
A: malaysia web design M: yevachow@gmail.com

vins2k.free.fr/prolo
D: vincent pucheux

www.alberguebolico.com
D: jorge mesa martín
M: jorge.mesa@gmail.com

www.qr5.com
D: matthew maaskant C: matthew maaskant P: matthew maaskant
A: draft tattoo M: info@drafttattoo.com

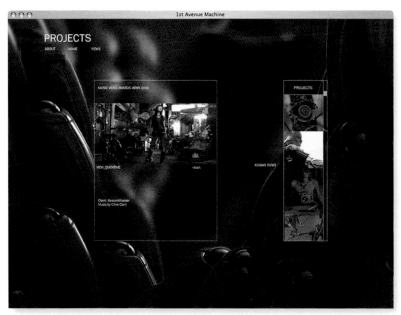

www.1stavemachine.com
D: arvind palep C: serge patzak P: serge patzak
A: 1st ave machine M: cm@1stavemachine.com

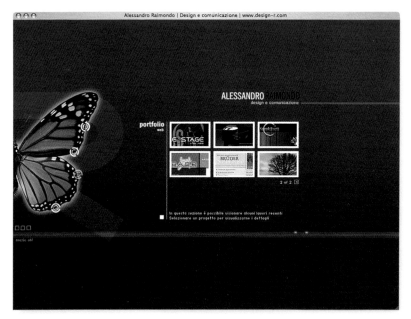

www.design-r.com
D: alessandro raimondo
M: info@design-r.com

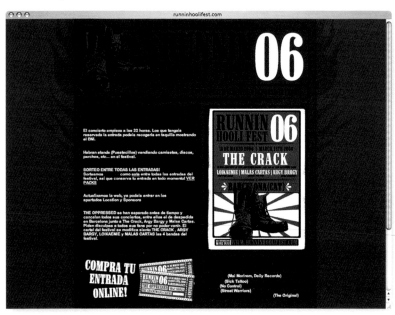

www.runninhoolifest.com
D: david sánchez fernández
A: subcultural design M: ruben@factorianorte.com

www.alazanto.org
D: kevin davis
M: kevin@alazanto.org

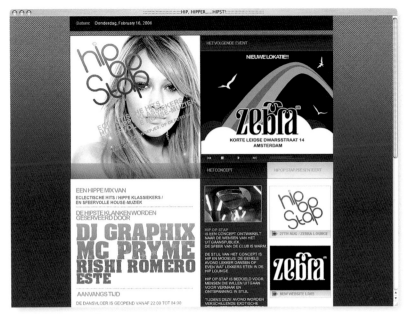

www.hipopstap.com/
D: glenn leming, steve tirbeni
A: bureau lift M: holla@liftyourself.nl

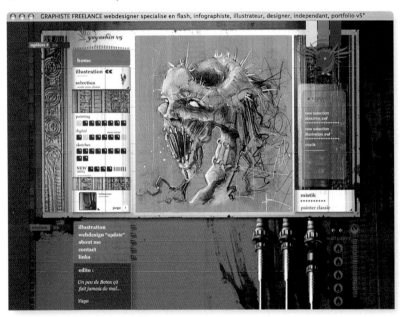

www.yayashin.com
D: bruno wagner C: bruno wagner P: bruno wagner
A: yayashin M: wag_bruno@yahoo.fr

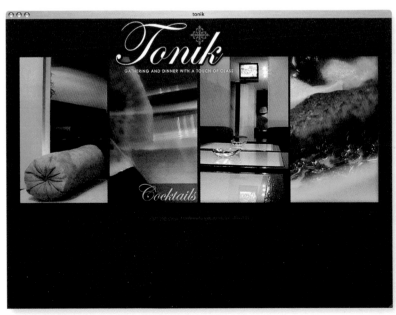

www.tonik.com.mx
D: jenaro diaz C: jenaro diaz P: jenaro diaz
A: djnr.net M: djnr@djnr.net

www.grupollanera.com
D: observer.es
M: news@observer.es

www.sommerhochzeit.hinrichs.de
D: chris alt C: demian grandt P: chris alt
A: chris alt design M: design@chrisalt.com

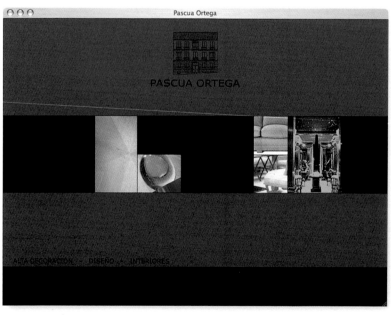

www.pascuaortega.com
D: francisco g. oria C: francisco g. oria P: francisco g. oria
A: go & asociados M: info@go-asociados.com

www.giemastruc.fr
D: giem astruc
M: www.giemastruc.fr

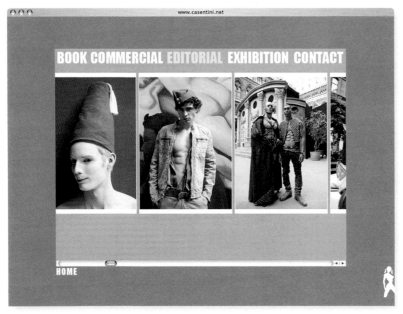

www.casentini.net
D: claudia casentini C: stefan gerhard draxler P: claudia casentini
A: claudia casentini M: claudia@casentini.net

www.conicos.com
D: cristian natalini P: conicos diseño + multimedia
A: conicos diseño + multimedia

www.lankwaifong.com
D: michael clough C: paul cheung
A: compelite ltd M: garry@compelite.net

www.jacoblangvad.com
D: e-types
M: hello@jacoblangvad.com

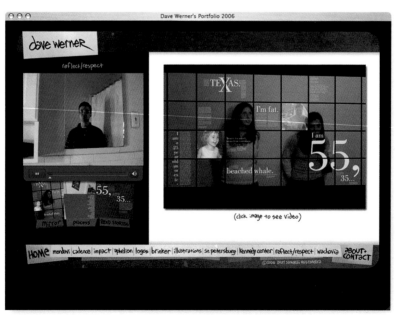

okaydave.com
D: dave werner
A: okay samurai multimedia M: davidwerner@gmail.com

www.contrecoups.com
D: eric duvauchelle
A: contre coups M: hello@contrecoups.com

olivier.danchin.neuf.fr
D: olivier danchin
M: olivier.danchin@neuf.fr

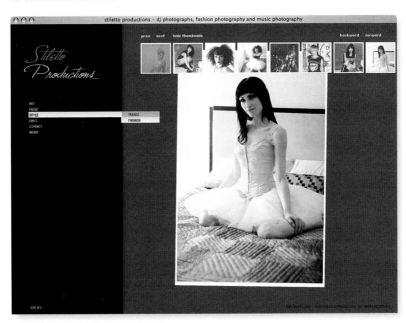

www.stilettoproductions.com
D: laszlo tandi C: laszlo tandi P: tandi and perrenoud
A: laszlo tandi M: elle@stilettoproductions.com

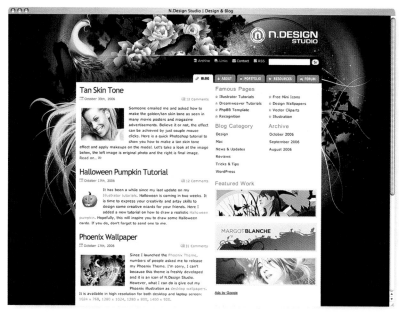

www.ndesign-studio.com
D: nick la
M: nick@ndesign-studio.com

www.woowoos.com
D: klaartje de buck C: thomas de groote P: chris de backer
A: www.woowoos.com M: chris@woowoos.com

www.thebutterflyeffect.dk
D: michael nielsen
M: michael@mcb.dk

www.draftmedia.de
D: thomas schröpfer
M: mail@draftmedia.de

www.poggiomolina.it
D: alessio papi
A: nextopen multimedia company M: www.nextopen.it

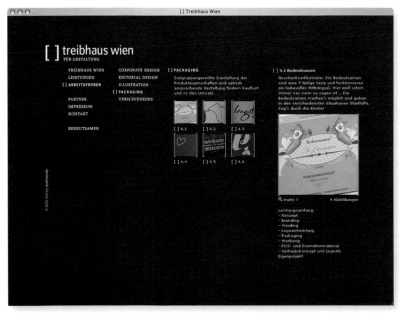

www.treibhaus-wien.at
D: tobias hildebrandt C: eye//candy P: eye//candy
A: eye//candy - agentur für consulting//kommunikation//design M: info@eyecandy.at

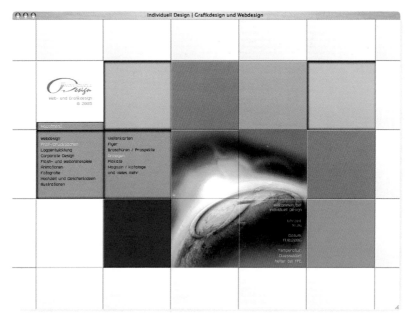

www.individuell-design.de
D: dieter bender C: dieter bender P: dieter bender
A: individuell-design M: web@individuell-design.de

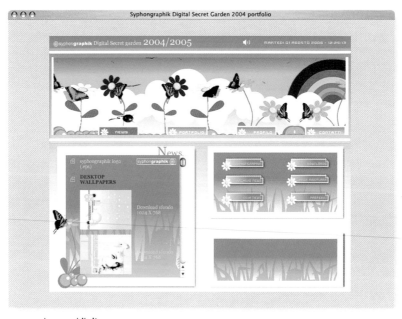

www.syphongraphik.it
D: gloria chiavistelli C: gloria chiavistelli P: gloria chiavistelli
A: syphongraphik M: gloria@syphongraphik.it

www.nonverbla.de
D: rasso hilber
A: rasso hilber | nonverbla M: rasso@nonverbla.de

www.steveleggat.com
D: steve leggat
M: me@steveleggat.com

www.micheleguitar.uni.cc
D: michele cricco C: michele cricco
A: crimic design studio M: info@crimic.com

www.ventilatorobjekte.de
D: diego gardón
M: www.diegogardon.de

www.grapamoda.com
D: ana abreu
A: cores ao cubo - gabinete de design M: info@coresaocubo.pt

www.emilianorodriguez.com.ar
D: emiliano rodríguez ruiz de gauna
A: emiliano rodríguez M: emi@emilianorodriguez.com.ar

www.partner-studio.com
D: juraj klaric C: juraj klaric P: juraj klaric
A: partner studio M: jure@partner-studio.com

www.inkieto.com
D: adrian carrasco C: inkieto P: inkieto
A: inkieto.com M: info@inkieto.com

www.cocoonmultimedia.com
D: merijn straathof
A: cocoon M: muhrijn@muhrijn.com

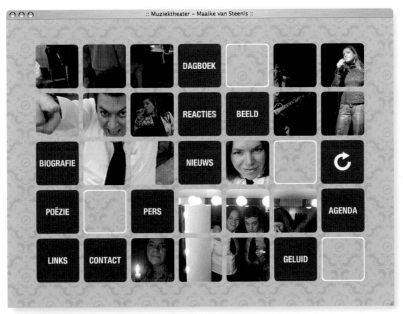

www.maaikevansteenis.nl
D: remco van der toorn C: remco van der toorn
A: studio plankton M: info@studioplankton.nl

www.oneasy.es
D: oneasy
M: oneasy@oneasy.es

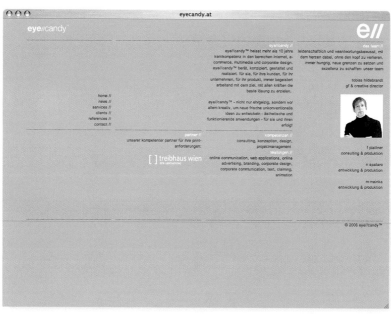

www.eyecandy.at
D: tobias hildebrandt C: eye//candy P: eye//candy
A: eye//candy - agentur für consulting//kommunikation//design M: info@eyecandy.at

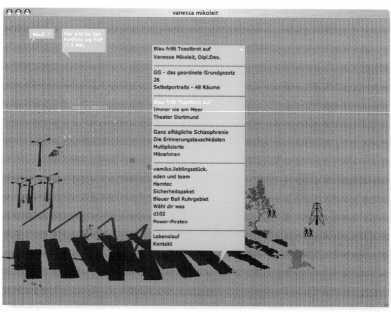

www.vanessa-mikoleit.de
D: vanessa mikoleit
M: www.vanessa-mikoleit.de

www.misipile.com
D: luka pensa C: domagoj pensa P: luka pensa
A: mis i pile M: info@misipile.com

www.choco.cc
D: tomz C: tristan
A: screenshot M: www.screenshot.be

www.dunil.pt
D: augusto lima C: augusto lima P: augusto lima
A: paulo correia M: www.paulocorreia.com

www.media-animation.be

D: benoît vrins C: sébastien denooz P: média animation
A: média animation M: b.vrins@media-animation.be

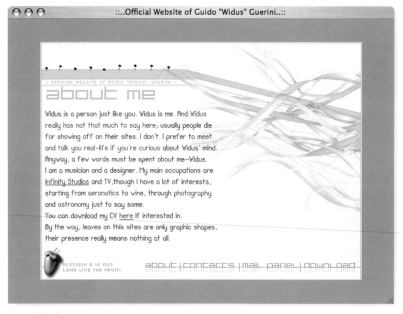

www.widus.it

D: guido guerini C: guido guerini P: guido guerini
A: www.infinitystudios.tv M: widus@widus.it

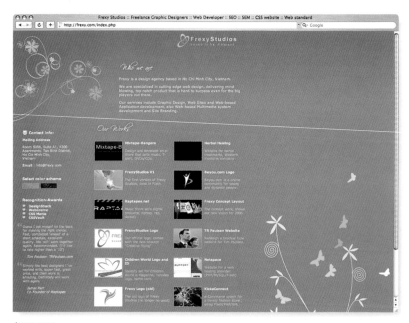

frexy.com

D: min tran
M: info@frexy.com

www.firstflash.net
D: massimo pavese C: peter krempl P: firstflash x-media labor, hamburg
A: firstflash x-media labor, hamburg M: team@firstflash.net

www.lookmysite.com
D: leonardo matias C: leonardo matias P: leonardo matias
A: lookmysite interactive M: www.lookmysite.com

www.maya-fashion.com
D: simone ertl, dominik mayer C: philipp wassibauer P: simone ertl, dominik mayer
A: maya inspiranto M: ciao@maya-fashion.com

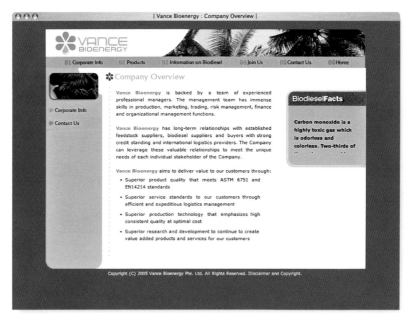

www.vancebioenergy.com
D: tracy bay P: joe chua
A: caffeine media pte ltd M: www.caffeine.com.sg

www.annastarkdesigns.com
D: anna m stark
A: anna stark designs M: info@annastarkdesigns.co.uk

www.opusmultipla.com.br/web/ccpr06/dombosco
D: rafael ribeiro C: bruno piza, fábio lonardoni P: fabiano cruz
A: opusmúltipla M: web@opusmultipla.com.br

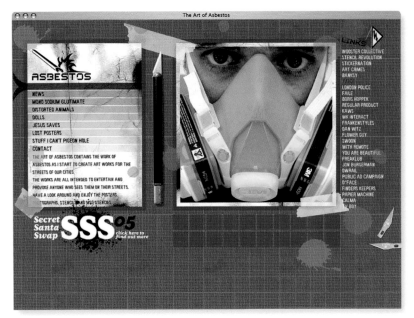

www.theartofasbestos.com
D: asbestos
M: me@theartofasbestos.com

www.sinelab.com
D: graham hutchings C: graham hutchings P: graham hutchings
A: sinelab M: graham@sinelab.co.uk

www.urbancollective.com
D: michael dawidowicz C: mitch ebdon P: michael dawidowicz
A: urban collective M: michael@urbancollective.com

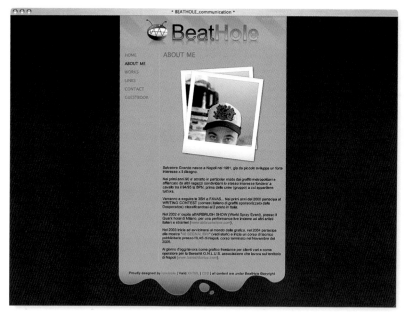

slork3sh.altervista.org/beathole/
D: salvatore grande, ciro visciano P: indelebile
A: beathole communication M: salvatoregrande@gmail.com

www.bastard.com.br
D: cláudia biss, augusto kraft, gilberto freitas C: e. hayashi, p. silva P: g. freitas
A: aliensdesign M: gilberto@aliensdesign.com.br

www.massgeschreinert.de
D: dennis rottler C: volker schweizer, dennis rottler P: rolf bouchama
A: cubus28 - sparkdesign M: www.cubus28.de - www.sparkdesign.de

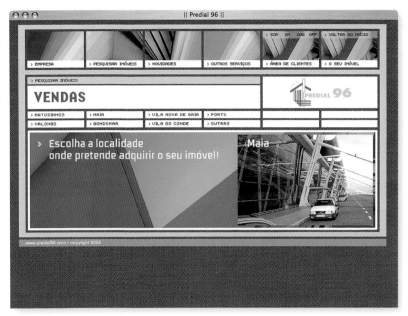

www.predial96.com
D: edgar afonso C: edgar afonso P: jorge cerqueira
A: deviusdesign M: edgar@deviusdesign.com

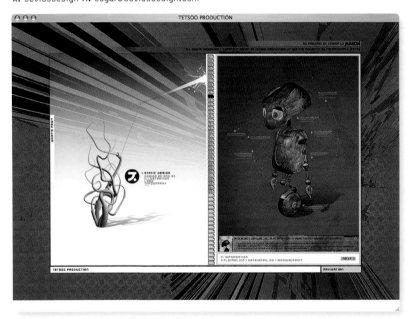

www.tetsoo.com
D: gregoire poget
A: tetsoo productions M: greg@tetsoo.com

www.carlos-polo.com
D: carlos polo C: carlos polo P: carlos polo
M: cpolo@carlos-polo.com

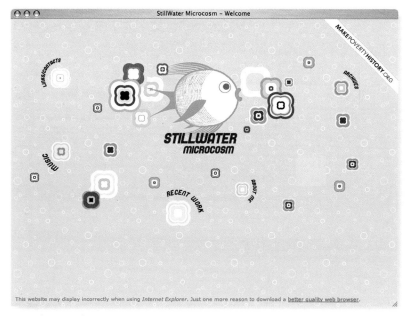

www.stillwater-microcosm.net
D: david bleja
M: dbleja@stillwater-microcosm.net

www.perfect99.com.my
D: eric lau ching lung C: ericanfly webstudio P: eric lau ching lung
A: ericanfly webstudio M: eric@ericanfly.com

www.infonomia.com
D: ignacio zorraquín C: bernat guitart grima P: infonomia
A: nomadesign M: www.nomadesign.org

www.1000visages.fr
D: cyril demars C: cyril demars P: 1000 visages
A: pixoil M: web2mc@wanadoo.fr

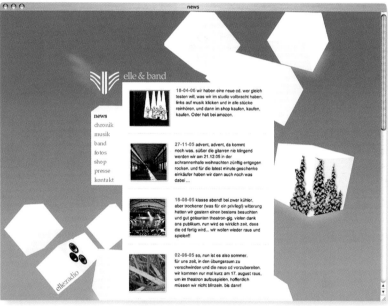

www.ellesound.de
D: severin brettmeister
M: severin@gutundwillig.de

www.plugster.ch
D: serge rau C: alaric mägerle P: serge rau
A: plugster M: serge.rau@plugster.ch

www.lambro-contracts.co.uk
D: sam marks C: tom newman P: lucas lynch
A: lucas lynch M: www.lucaslynch.com

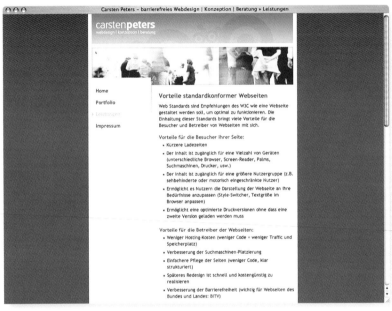

carsten-peters.net
D: carsten peters C: carsten peters
A: carsten peters M: cp@carsten-peters.net

www.matthias-maschmann.de
D: dirk heinemann C: henning lehfeldt P: matthias maschmann
A: nordisch:com M: dirk.heinemann@nordisch.com

www.behindthescenes.de
D: guido eichhoff C: guido eichhoff P: guido eichhoff
A: artboxx M: guido@artboxx.net

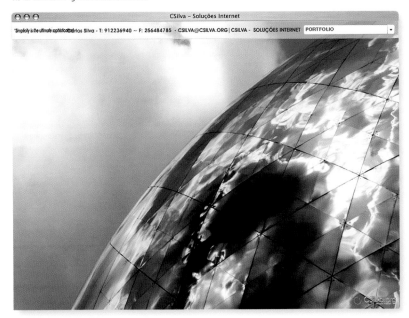

www.csilva.org
D: carlos silva
A: csilva.org M: www.csilva.org

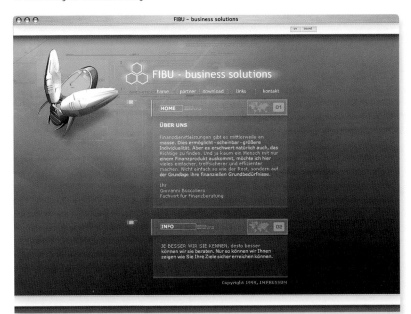

www.investmentshaus.name
D: giovanni buccoliero C: giovanni buccoliero
M: giovanni_buccoliero@web.de or www.fibu.name

www.doismaisdois.com
D: diogo melo C: diogo melo P: diogo melo
A: doismaisdois.com M: dmelo@hotmail.com

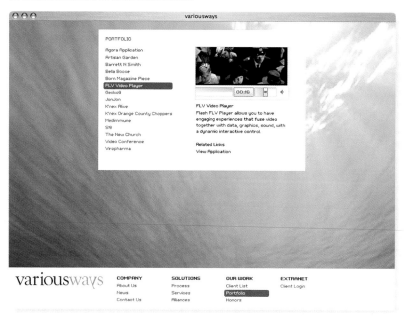

www.variousways.com
D: jon montenegro
A: variousways inc. M: info@variousways.com

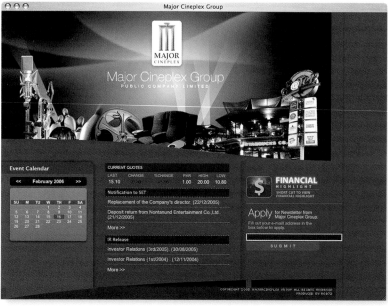

corporate.majorcineplex.com
D: s. sirimaskasem C: w. suksangworn, peerapong, chaivoot, somphong P: sirimaskasem
A: rgb72 M: www.rgb72.com

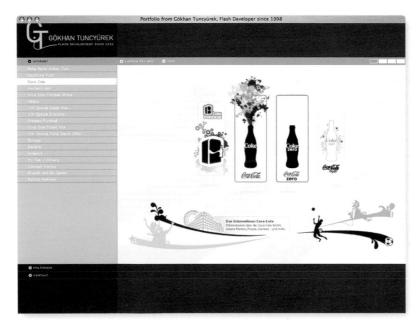

www.deltatransform.com
D: veysel önder C: gökhan tuncyürek P: gökhan tuncyürek
A: flash development gökhan tuncyürek M: flash@deltatransform.com

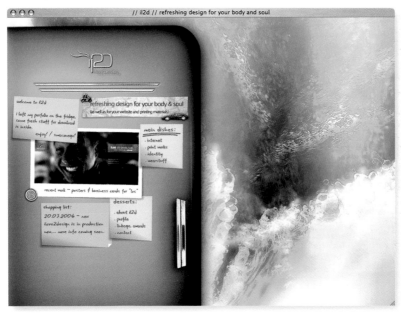

www.ilove2design.com
D: maciek czmuda C: maciek czmuda
A: ilove2design M: futer@ilove2design.com

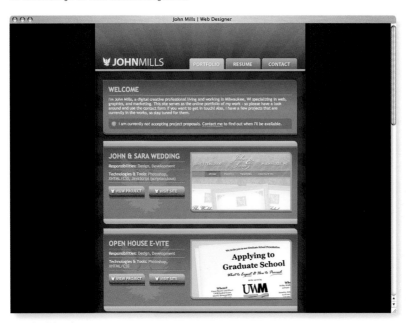

www.iamjohnmills.com
D: john mills
M: me@johnmills.us

www.sndk.no
D: rune wold , irene holmen C: rune wold P: rune wold
A: sndk as M: info@sndk.info

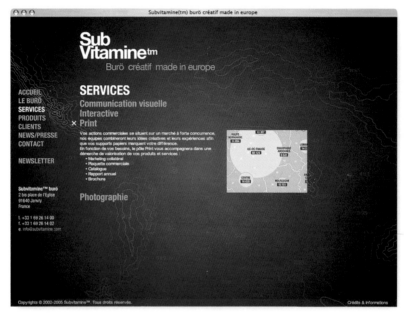

www.subvitamine.com
D: thomas desbouvrie C: yannick stroobants P: olivier lacombe
A: subvitamine(tm) M: info@subvitamine.com

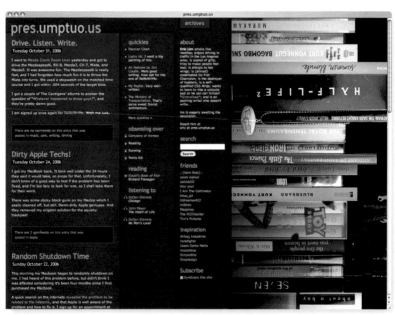

pres.umptuo.us
D: eric lim
M: eric@pres.umptuo.us

www.stackopolis.com
D: lee pennington C: iain lobb P: rick palmer
A: bloc M: hello@blocmedia.com

www.vincent-vella.com
D: vincent vella
M: info@vincent-vella.com

www.ondaline-adv.com
D: gabriele gargiulo C: gabriele gargiulo P: ondaline adv
A: ondaline adv M: gabriele@ondaline-adv.com

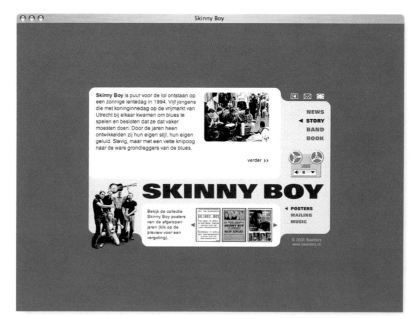

www.skinnyboy.nl
D: michiel stoop C: michiel stoop P: skinny boy
A: beelders M: skinnyboy@beelders.nl

www.turistrela.pt
D: telmo de campos martins C: luis dias P: joão feitor
A: lobby productions M: geral@lobbyproductions.com

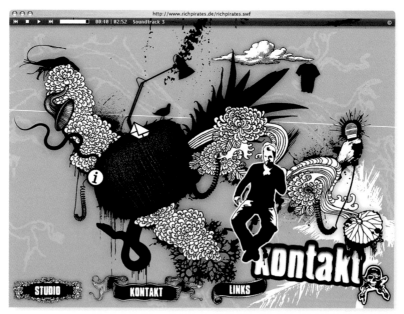

www.richpirates.de
D: andreas kretzer C: andreas kretzer P: andreas kretzer
A: kretzer - architektur und szenenbild M: kontakt@architekturetc.de

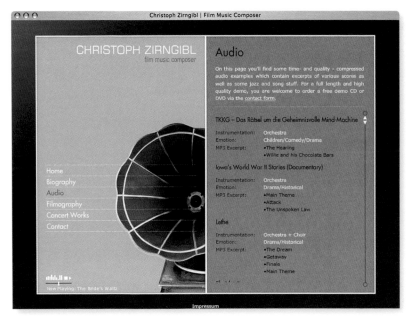

www.neverplayedmusic.com
D: bernd kugler C: bernd kugler P: bernd kugler
A: reihel M: www.reihel.com

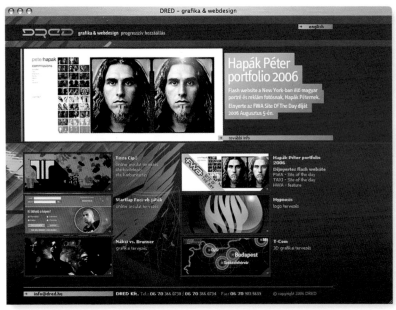

www.dred.hu
D: imre ferenczi, zoltan szalay
A: dred M: info@dred.hu

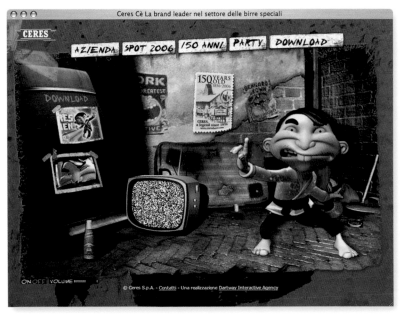

www.ceresbeer.com
D: danilo rolle C: danilo rolle
A: dartway M: drolle@dartway.com

www.pixelhood.com
D: julius bencko C: julius bencko P: julius bencko
A: pixelhood twisted designs M: juice@pixelhood.com

www.gardunoarquitectos.com
D: cecilia cortés contreras
A: creatividad marketing y diseño s.c. M: ccortes@cmdcreativo.com

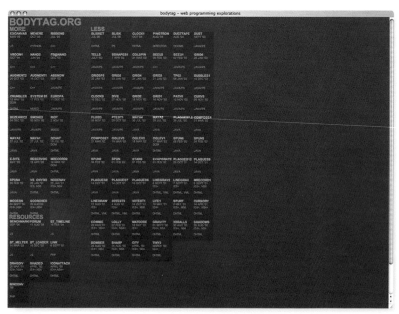

bodytag.org
D: glen murphy
M: glenmurphy.com

www.moosesyrup.com
D: mike hansen
A: moosesyrup M: mikeh@moosesyrup.com

www.mindflood.com
D: chris lund, noah costello C: chris kief
A: mindflood M: info@mindflood.com

www.bupla.com
D: bupla
M: contact@bupla.com

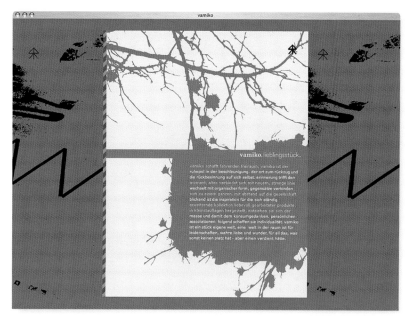

www.vamiko.de
D: vanessa mikoleit
M: vanessa@vanessa-mikoleit.de

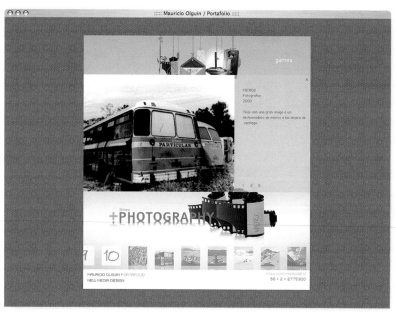

www.medialab.cl
D: mauricio olguin C: mauricio olguin P: mauricio olguin
A: medialab.cl M: mauricio@medialab.cl

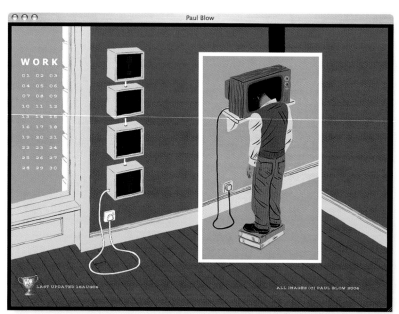

www.paulblow.com
D: paul blow
M: paul@paulblow.com

www.pfw-online.de
D: oliver wienand C: franz josef drewer-gutland P: franz josef drewer-gutland
A: nettrix multi media M: info@nettrix.de

www.danija-shoes.com
D: andrius kuciauskas C: domas juknevicius P: andrius kuciauskas
A: deformgroup M: info@deform-group.com

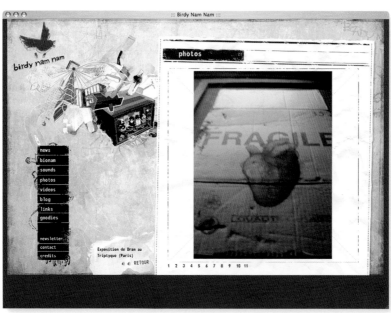

www.birdynamnam.com
D: sonia borsarelli C: emmanuel saccoccini P: grouek, birdy nam nam
A: grouek M: grouekies@grouek.com, magnetikproductions@free.fr

www.jazzve.com
D: aghasi aghabalyan C: george aznavouryan, andrey vanyan P: aghasi aghabalyan
A: fluger M: fluger@fluger.com

guilago.se
D: tobias nilsson C: tobias nilsson P: tobias nilsson
A: guilago M: tobias@guilago.se

www.milchkleid.de
D: judith sombray C: marc bauer
A: milchkleid illustration M: schreib@milchkleid.de

www.nineoff.com
D: ricardo contreras
A: halfpastnine srl M: info@halfpastnine.it

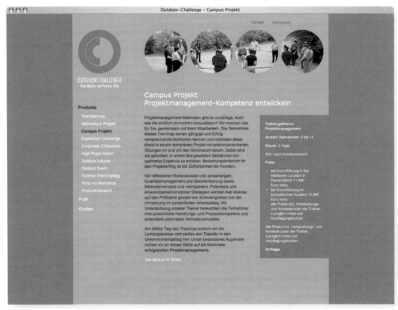

www.outdoor-challenge.de
D: david weber C: david weber P: david weber
A: d++ M: info@dplusplus.de

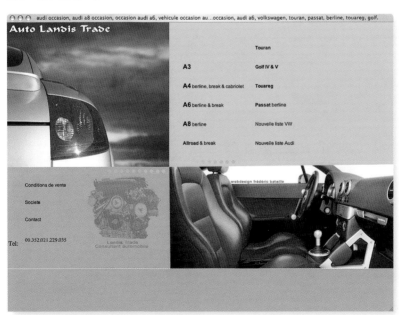

www.auto-landis-trade.com
D: frederic bataille
A: fbnet M: fred.ba@free.fr

www.mutanthands.com
D: james wignall C: james wignall P: james wignall
A: mutanthands M: james@mutanthands.com

www.martacorcho.com
D: marta corcho tarifa C: bernardo jimenez toman P: marta corcho tarifa
A: equilibriografico M: contacto@martacorcho.com

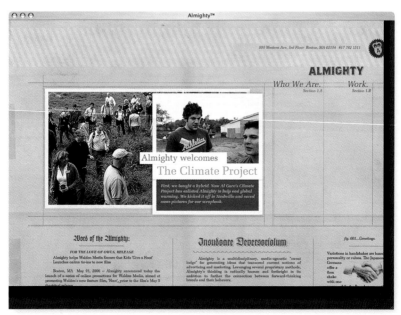

almightyboston.com
D: j. polevy, rj evans, i. fitzpatrick, c. smith C: i. fitzpatrick, p. larrow P: m. charde
A: almighty M: matthew.charde@almightyboston.com

www.emilykeegin.com
D: wyeth hansen, emily keegin
M: emily@emilykeegin.com

www.stgu.pl
D: pawel przybyl C: pawel przybyl P: stgu
A: pawel przybyl, siedemzero.com M: info@stgu.pl , siedemzero@wp.pl

www.robertreich.de
D: robert reich
M: mail@robertreich.de

www.visuellerorgasmus.de/pixeltown/pixeltown.htm
D: maik sander, matias roskos, frank feldmann C: maik sander P: matias roskos
A: visualorgasm.de M: frank@visualorgasm.de

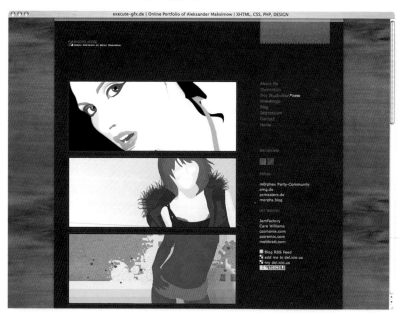

www.execute-gfx.de
D: aleksander maksimow C: aleksander maksimow P: aleksander maksimow
A: execute-gfx M: ihunte@gmail.com

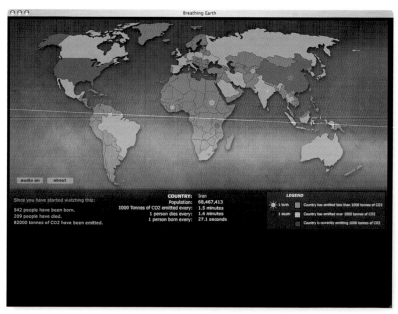

breathingearth.net
D: david bleja
M: dbleja@stillwater-microcosm.net

www.filemeaway.com
D: josh lehman
A: lehman design M: info@joshlehman.com

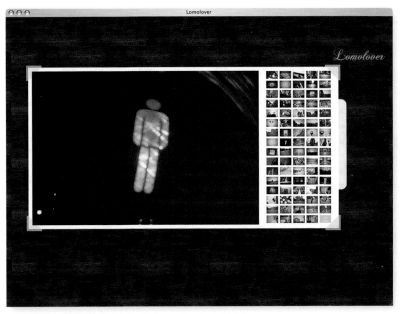

www.lomolover.com
D: florian mueller
A: bonsai prod. M: florian@lomolover.com

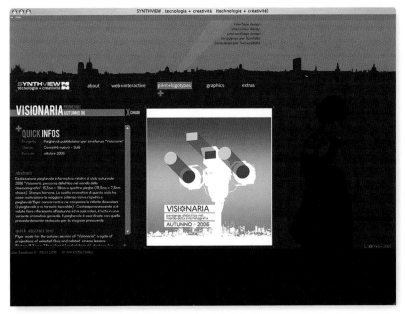

www.synthview.com
D: jan tonellato
M: info@synthview.com

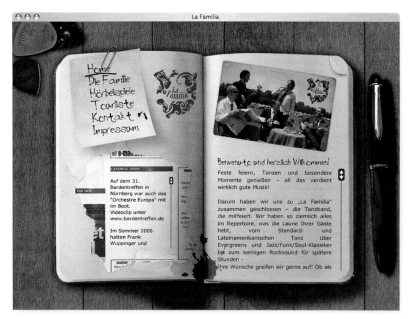

www.familia-online.de
D: bernd kugler C: bernd kugler P: bernd kugler
A: reihel M: www.reihel.com

www.albergo-laposta.it
D: riccardo ghignoni C: riccardo ghignoni
A: sintra consulting s.r.l. M: r.ghignoni@sintraconsulting.it

www.drawingart.org
D: miro koljanin C: miro koljanin P: miro koljanin
A: drawingart M: info@drawingart.org

www.kioskstudio.net
D: ratko jagodic C: hrvoje vranekovic P: ratko jagodic
A: kiosk studio M: kontakt@kioskstudio.net

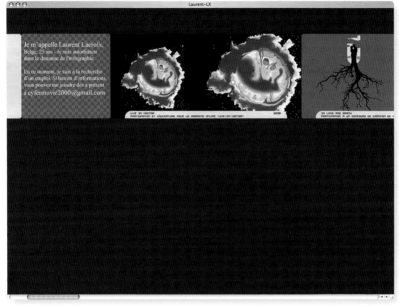

www.laurent-lx.be
D: laurent lacroix
M: cyfermovie2000@gmail.com

iso50.com
D: scott hansen C: dusty brown P: scott hansen
A: iso50 M: hello@iso50.com

www.maisonapresminuit.net
D: andrea bianchi C: andrea bianchi P: andrea bianchi
A: maison après minuit M: andrea@maisonapresminuit.net

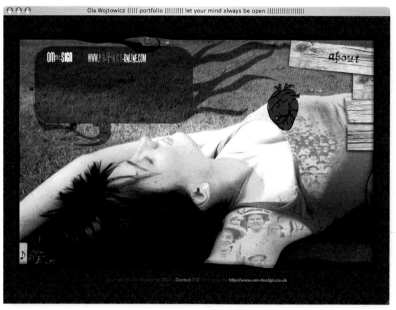

www.olawojtowicz.com
D: ola wojtowicz C: marek matias P: ola wojtowicz, marek matias
A: omdesign M: ola@om-design.co.uk

agencynet.com
D: r. lent, g. bugda, m. pereira, j. princz C: lent, princz, m. penela, brown P: lent, fullman
A: agencynet M: bizdev@agencynet.com

www.boutique-dammann.fr
D: sokovision
M: eric.marillet@sokovision.com

www.kezako.be
D: sandy lemoine C: sandy lemoine P: sandy lemoine
A: kezako M: sandy@kezako.be

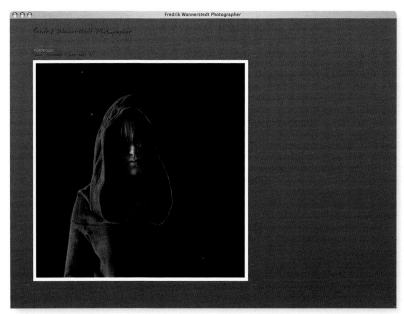

www.wannerstedt.com
D: andreas wannerstedt C: andreas wannerstedt P: andreas wannerstedt
A: foedus M: andreas@foedus.se

www.mylkhead.com
D: jeff finley
A: go media M: jeff@mylkhead.com

www.alphanumeric.cz
D: jan brasna
A: alphanumeric M: posta@alphanumeric.cz

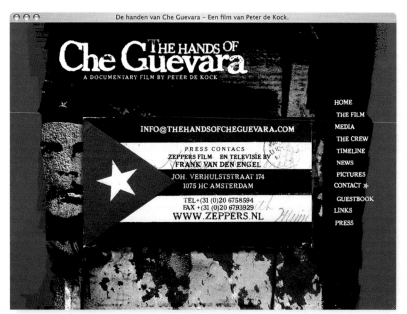

www.thehandsofcheguevara.com
D: michiel corten C: bart waalen
A: bruut ontwerp M: www.bruut.com

www.keo.be
D: kristof van rentergem C: kristof van rentergem P: kristof van rentergem
A: weblounge M: www.weblounge.be

www.dqbooks.com
D: pierrick calvez
A: www.1h05.com M: dqbooks@1h05.com

www.1000needles.com
D: magnus kjäll
M: magnus@1000needles.com

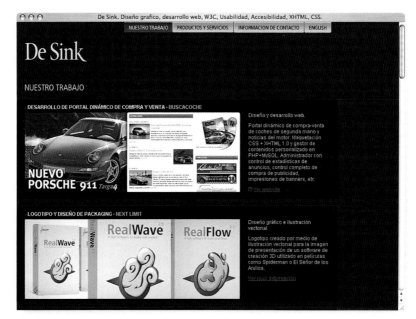

www.desink.com
D: miguel angel benitez, david pareja C: raul ledo
A: de sink, c.b. M: info@desink.com

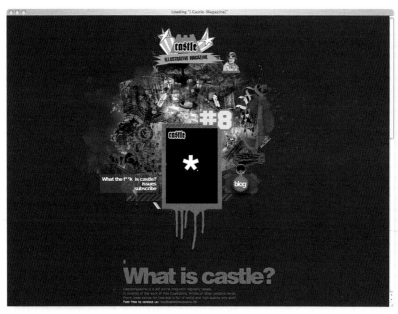

www.castlemagazine.de
D: michael matthias, patrick hartl C: ray tischler P: michael matthias, patrick hartl
A: michael matthias, patrick hartl M: me@castlemagazine.de

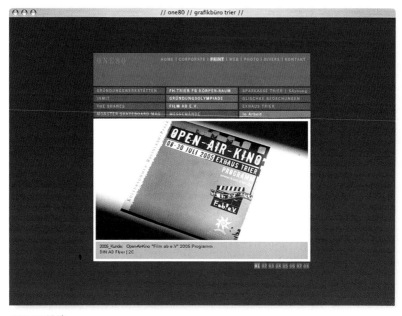

www.one80.de
D: a. goltz
M: www.one80.de

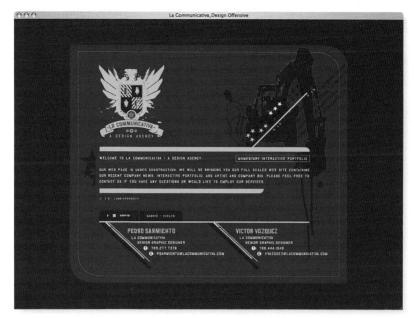

www.lacommunicativa.com
D: pedro sarmiento C: pedro sarmiento P: victor vazquez
A: la communicativa - a design agency M: psarmiento@lacommunicativa.com

www.troubleyn.be
D: marcel lennartz, kim matthé C: kim matthé P: troubleyn, jan fabre
A: monsieur moiré M: www.monsieurmoire.com

liquidassets.liquisoft.com
D: ryan ford C: ryan ford

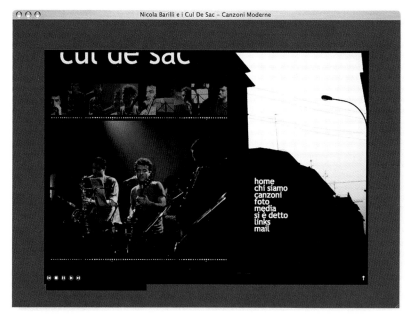

www.cul-de-sac.it
D: pino ceniccola C: pino ceniccola P: pino ceniccola
A: pinit M: me@pinit.it

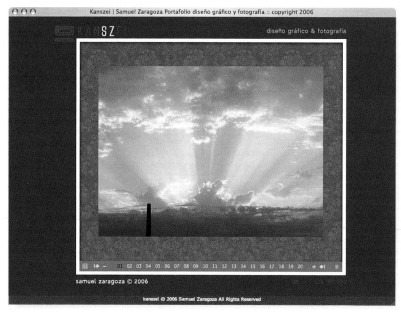

www.kanszei.com
D: samuel zaragoza
M: samu@kanszei.com

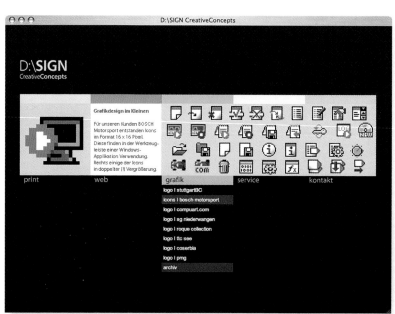

www.dsign.de
D: stefan behringer C: jürgen wunderle
A: d:\sign creativeconcepts M: contact@dsign.de

www.estatemanagement.sk
D: michal bartko **C:** michal bartko
A: webdesignfactory **M:** factory@webdesignfactory.sk

www.ringvlaamseopera.be
D: marcel lennartz, kim matthé **C:** kim matthé **P:** vlaamse opera (ivo van hove)
A: monsieur moiré **M:** www.monsieurmoire.com

www.umair.com
D: umair siddiqui
A: creative dimensions **M:** umair@umair.com

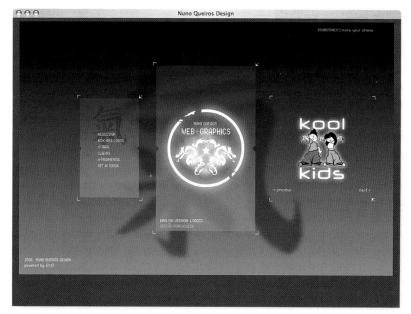

www.nunoqueiros.com
D: nuno queiros
A: nuno queiros design M: info@nunoqueiros.com

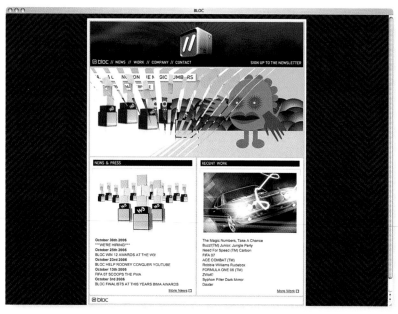

www.blocmedia.com
D: rick palmer C: steve hayes
A: bloc M: hello@blocmedia.com

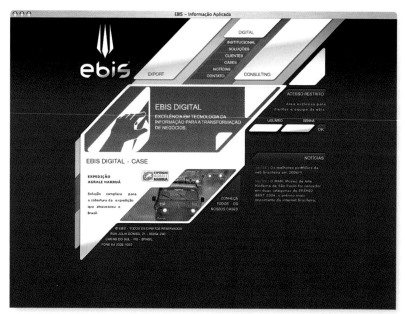

www.ebis.com.br
D: alisson laschuk
A: ebis M: contato@alisson.com.br

www.quimeia.com
D: daniel garcia del moral C: daniel garcia del moral P: daniel garcia del moral
A: quimeia studio M: daniel@quimeia.com

www.jerzyk.art.pl
D: mateusz jerzyk
M: mateusz@jerzyk.art.pl

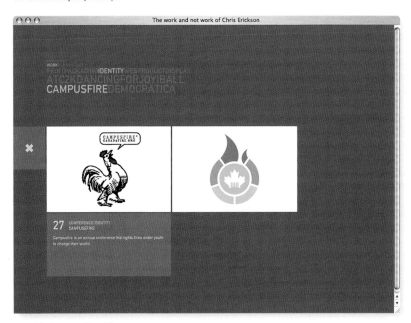

www.kindnessandhumility.com
D: chris erickson C: chris erickson P: chris erickson
A: kindness and humility M: chris@kindnessandhumility.com

fornaldesign.pl
D: przemek fornal, magda fornal C: pawel stanislawczuk P: przemek fornal
A: to design - design studio M: info@fornaldesign.pl

www.webberz.it
D: marco marini
A: webber M: marco.m@webberz.it

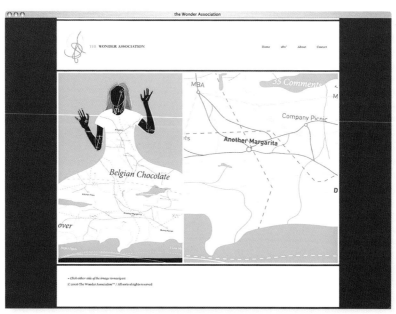

wonderassociation.com
D: helgi p. einarsson C: benjamin mermaid
A: the wonder association M: office@wonderassociation.com

www.bruut.com
D: michiel corten C: bart waalen
A: bruut ontwerp M: www.bruut.com

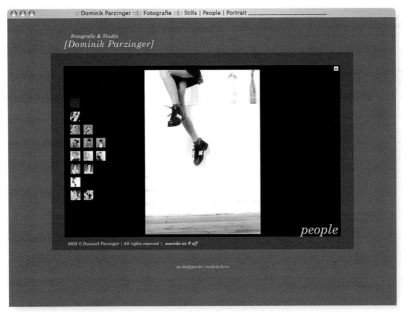

www.parzinger-dominik.de
D: severin brettmeister
A: fa-ro marketing gmbh M: info@fa-ro.de

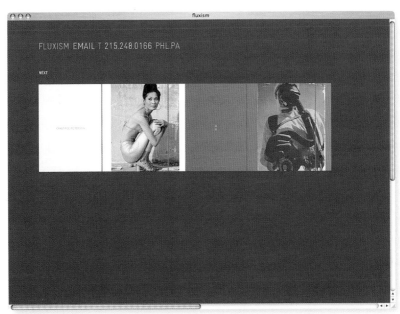

www.fluxism.com
D: jon rohrer
A: fluxism M: mail@fluxism.com

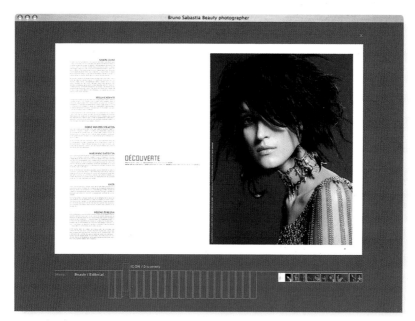

www.sabastia.com
D: akim benrezzag C: vincent le badezet P: bruno sabastia
A: sabastia M: b@sabastia.com

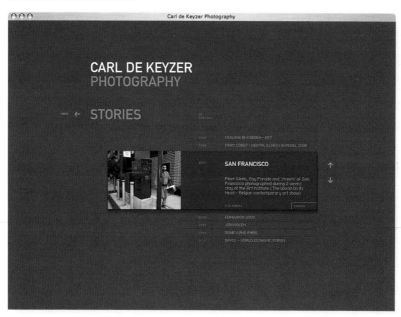

www.carldekeyzer.com
D: pascal leroy C: pascal leroy P: pascal leroy
A: group94 M: carl@carldekeyzer.com

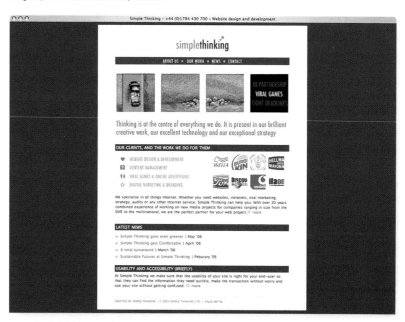

www.simplethinking.co.uk
D: richard hiscutt C: richard hiscutt, alister lilley P: simple thinking ltd.
A: simple thinking ltd. M: contact@simplethinking.co.uk

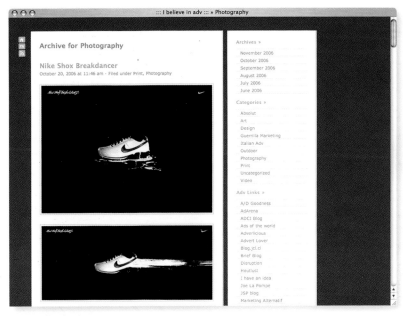

www.ibelieveinadv.com
D: filippo solimena C: filippo solimena, lokesh dhakar, oriol P: filippo solimena
M: filippo@ibelieveinadv.com

www.marjolijn.net
D: marjolijn kamphuis P: marjolijn kamphuis
M: marjolijn.net@gmail.com

www.kalchmann.com
D: alexander kremecek C: alexander kremecek P: alexander kremecek
A: diamonddogs webconsulting M: www.diamonddogs.cc

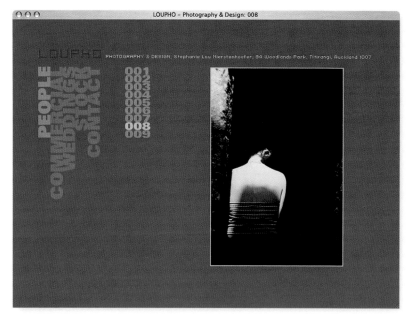

www.loupho.com
D: claudia vasel C: dierk roeder
A: hoffnungsträger - visuelle kommunikation M: www.die-hoffnungstraeger.de

www.entwicklungsagentur.de
D: a. goltz, w.schmitz C: m. thomm
A: www.one80.de M: agoltz@one80.de

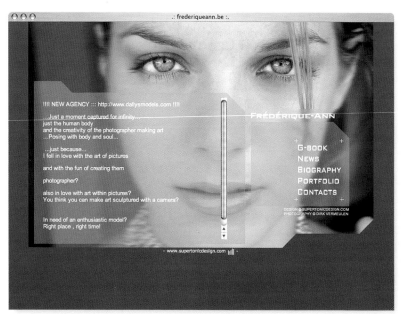

www.frederique-ann.be
D: tim verhees C: tim verhees P: tim verhees
A: supertonic design M: info@supertonicdesign.com

www.bam-b.com
D: faiyaz jafri
M: faiyaz@bam-b.com

www.redreactor.com
D: carl bender C: c. bender P: c. bender
A: red reactor M: carl@redreactor.com

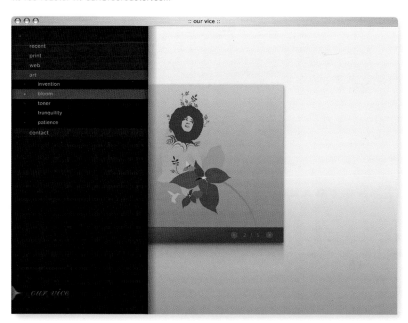

www.ourvice.com
D: sean obrien , destin young C: destin young
A: ourvice M: throttle@ourvice.com

www.hungout.com
D: jordan stone, martin hughes
A: wefail.com M: ronnie@hungout.com

www.bastardgraphics.com
D: julien rivoire C: julien rivoire P: julien rivoire
A: bastardgraphics M: info@bastardgraphics.com

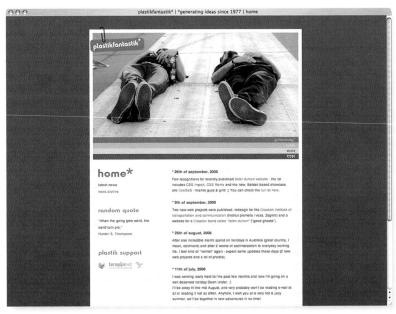

plastikfantastik.net
D: sasa huzjak C: sasa huzjak P: sasa huzjak
A: plastikfantastik* M: plastikfantastik.net

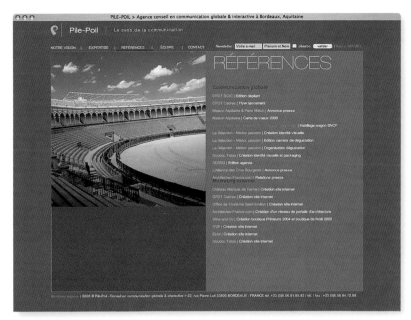

www.pile-poil.com
D: pile-poil
M: contact@pile-poil.com

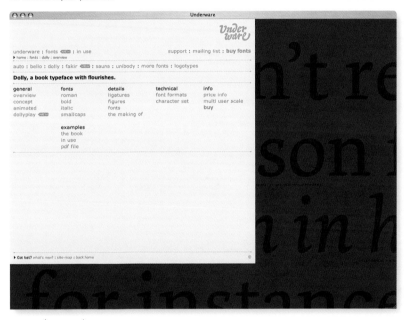

www.underware.nl
D: underware
M: info@underware.nl

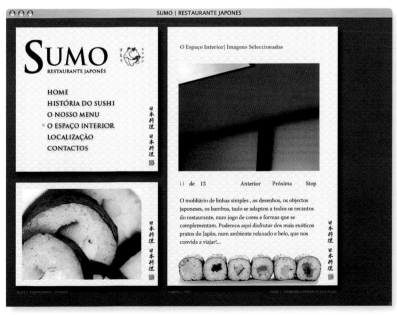

www.restaurantesumo.com
D: nuno horta
A: nhdesign M: geral@nunohorta.com

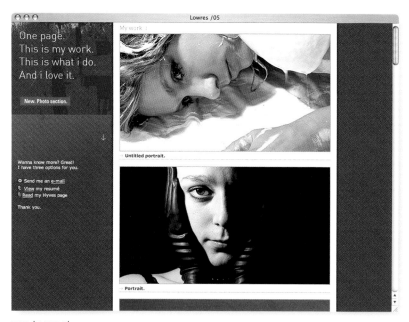

www.lowres.nl
D: jop quirindongo
M: jop@lowres.nl

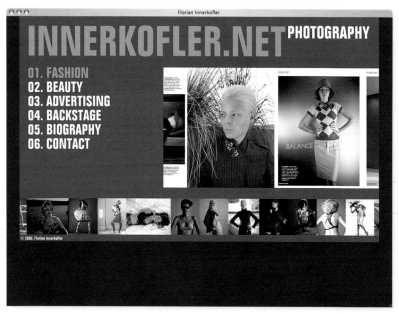

www.innerkofler.net
D: innerkofler florian C: winkler dirk, www.gdnm.com P: innerkofler florian, winkler dirk
A: innerkofler florian M: studio@innerkofler.net

www.keoshi.com
D: filipe varela
A: keoshi.com M: keoshi@keoshi.com

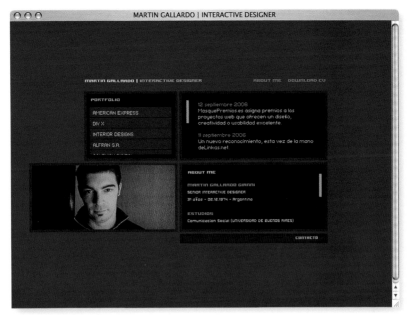

www.martingallardo.com.ar
D: martín gallardo
M: contacto@martingallardo.com.ar

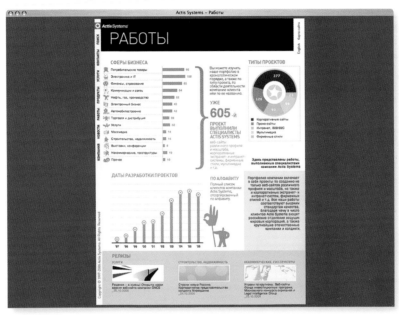

www.actis.ru
D: valery fironov, alexander kudryavtsev, ilya sivov P: alexey antonov
A: actis systems M: info@actis.ru

www.x3studios.com
D: stefan szakal, sorin bechira C: catalin saveanu, calin iepure P: stefan szakal
A: x3 studios M: info@x3studios.com

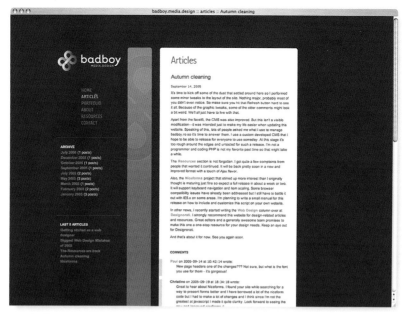

www.badboy.ro
D: lucian slatineanu
A: badboy.media.design M: badboy@badboy.ro

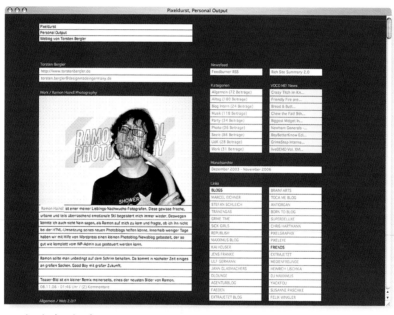

www.torstenbergler.de
D: torsten bergler
M: torsten.bergler@designmadeingermany.de

www.visualghetto.net
D: bahadir canberk C: bahadir canberk
M: feed@visualghetto.net

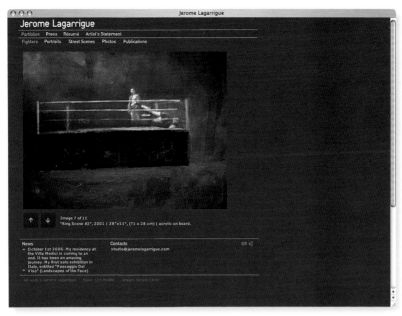

www.jeromelagarrigue.com
D: elliott golden C: elliott golden, anwar montasir P: elliott golden
A: simple circle llc M: studio@simplecircle.net

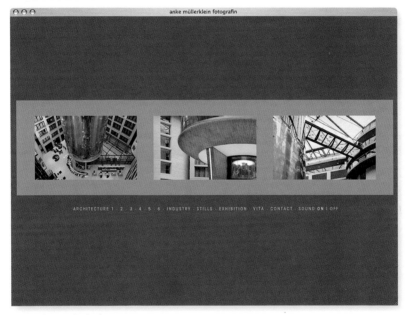

www.anke-muellerklein.com
D: dorothee bächle C: dorothee bächle P: anke müllerklein
A: graphics4web M: info@graphics4web

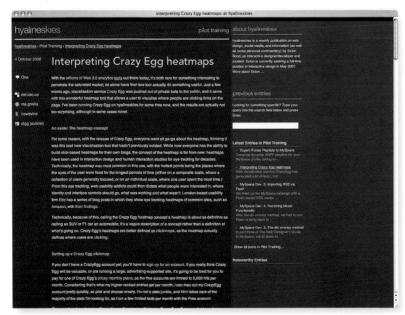

hyalineskies.com
D: eston bond C: eston bond
M: eston@hyalineskies.com

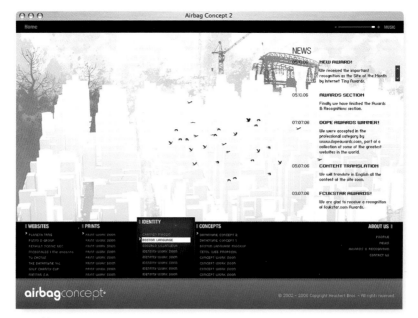

www.airbagconcept.com.ar
D: alex heuchert C: alex heuchert P: alex heuchert
A: airbag concept M: info@airbagconcept.com.ar

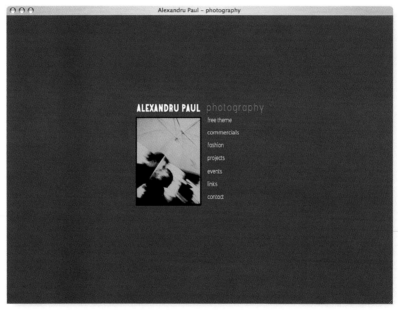

www.alexandrupaul.com
D: oleg tishkovets C: gheorghe serban
A: alexandru paul srl M: paul@alexandrupaul.com

www.juliafullerton-batten.com
D: bite digital
M: julia@juliafb.com

jonkeegan.com
D: jon keegan
M: jon@jonkeegan.com

www.lucasomaini.com
D: luca somaini
M: contact@lucasomaini.com

chunkid.nl
D: martijn de beijer C: dirk bertels P: frank rosenhart
A: chunk|id M: chunkid.nl

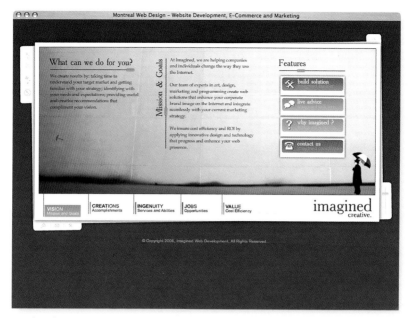

www.imagined.ca
D: matthew higgins et al C: matthew higgins et al P: michael whitham
A: imagined creative M: info@imagined.ca

www.spokes.nl
D: lesley-ann hania C: tennie lanslots P: lesley-ann hania, lotte staats
A: lawless & lotski design M: www.lawlesslotski.nl

www.diepmandegraaf.nl
D: ale van der ploeg C: edwin de vries P: ale van der ploeg
A: addsite internet M: www.addsite.nl

shadowtones.net
D: oxana diakonashvili C: dmitri goutnik
M: oxana@shadowtones.net

www.meridiany.com
D: orshak myroslav C: eugene arefyev
A: mif design studio M: www.mifdesign.com

seofirmatlanta.com
D: kris C: kinard
A: scs atlanta

www.agatha.com.br
D: eugênio oliveira C: eugênio oliveira P: eugênio oliveira
A: teaching ´n training M: eoliveira@teachingntraining.com

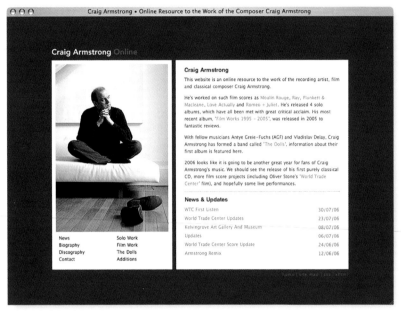

www.craigarmstrongonline.com
D: adam lloyd C: adam lloyd P: adam lloyd
A: vanillapearl M: adam@vanillapearl.com

www.steube-art-atelier.de
D: doris steube C: friederike mühleck P: doris steube
A: steube-art-atelier M: info@muehleck-designbuero.de

www.briancasseyphotographer.com.au
D: karl hedner C: karl hedner P: jesper hedner
A: julian kommunikation M: www.julian.se

www.brunocoppola.com.ar
D: bruno matías cóppola
A: bruno cóppola diseño M: info@brunocoppola.com.ar

www.collaweb.it
D: davide sossi , daniele de batté
A: artiva design M: www.artiva.it

www.ilovedzn.com
D: andré assalino
M: info@ilovedzn.com

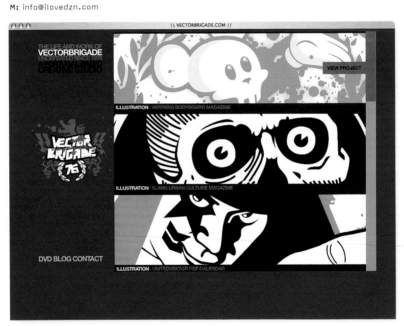

www.vectorbrigade.com
D: nuno baltazar C: nuno baltazar P: nuno baltazar
A: vectorbrigade M: studio@vectorbrigade.com

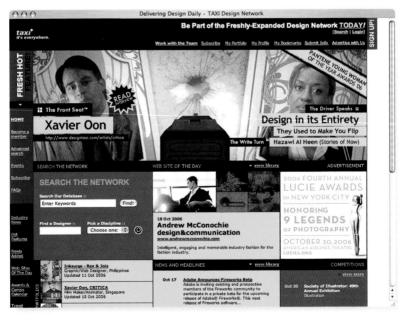

www.designtaxi.com
D: alex goh k.c. C: ting zien lee
A: hills creative arts M: media@hillscreativearts.com

www.showoff-films.com
D: sofia vitor C: wolfgang borgsmuller P: sofia vitor
A: aftamina M: www.aftamina.pt

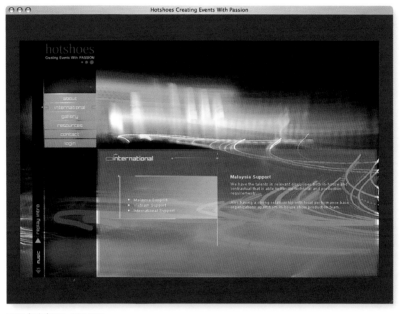

www.hotshoes.com.my
D: robin liew C: robin liew, lek
A: gxm studio M: info@gxmstudio.com

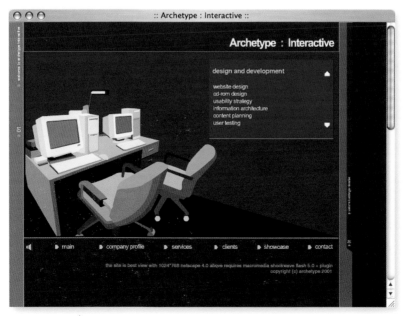

www.a-i.com.hk/ai_v1
D: john wu, benny luk P: john wu
A: archetype interactive limited M: info@a-i.com.hk

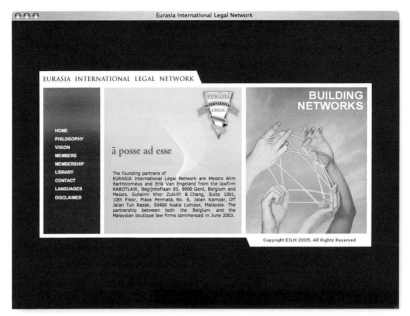

www.eurasialegalnetwork.com
D: nidzam harjoh P: idzhar ibrahim
A: malaysian internet resources (mir) M: www.mir.com.my

www.starduck.org
D: fernando fuentes C: fernando fuentes P: starduck.org
A: starduck.org M: starduck@starduck.org

www.shinybinary.com
D: nik ainley
A: shinybinary M: nik@shinybinary.com

www.danlindop.co.uk
D: dan lindop
A: dan lindop web design M: hello@danlindop.co.uk

www.bluegraph.com
D: cyril casagrande
M: cyril.casagrande@bluegraph.com

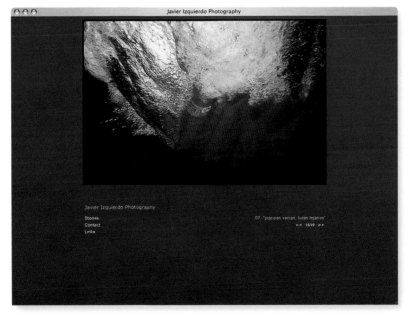

www.javierportfolio.com
D: javier izquierdo
A: mi casa M: javierportfolio@hotmail.com

www.mfran.com
D: alberto álvarez C: daniel sánchez P: alberto álvarez
A: dealfil estudio M: www.dealfil.com

djstandox.com
D: monkeydesign.nl
M: info@monkeydesign.nl

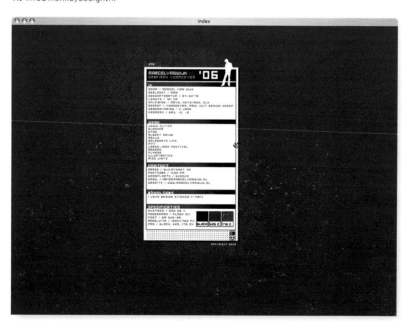

www.marcelvanwijk.nl
D: marcel van wijk
A: marcelvanwijk.nl M: info@marcelvanwijk.nl

www.gizwizstudio.com
D: tee ewe jin C: khaw chin siong P: gizwiz studio
A: gizwiz studio M: ewejin@gizwizstudio.com

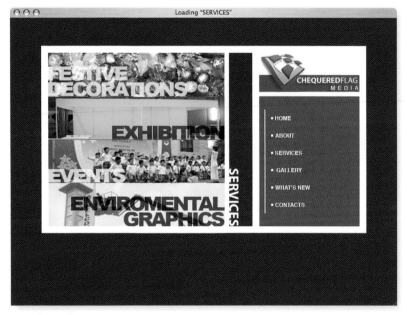

www.cflagmedia.com
D: david chit C: david chit P: felix oking
A: chequered flag media M: felix.oking@cflagmedia.com

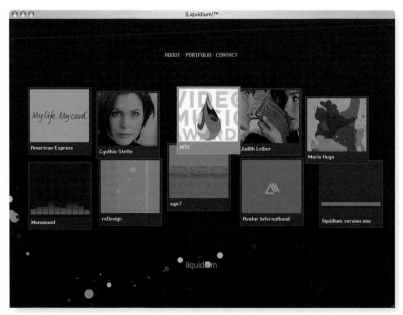

www.liquidium.com
D: adriaan schölvinck C: adriaan schölvinck P: adriaan schölvinck
A: liquidium M: adriaan@liquidium.com

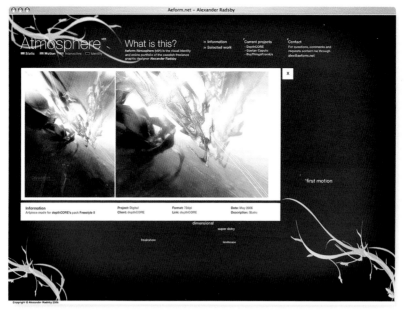

www.aeform.net
D: alexander radsby
M: aeform.net

www.eyewake.com
D: gaston siciliano C: eyewake design force development team P: eyewake design force
A: eyewake design force, inc. M: info@eyewake.com

www.bartels-werkhaus.de
D: matthias klegraf C: engine productions medienproduktion P: sevn koeln
A: sevn koeln M: www.sevn.de

www.dasol-music.com
D: malte müller C: malte müller
A: electricgecko M: www.electricgecko.de

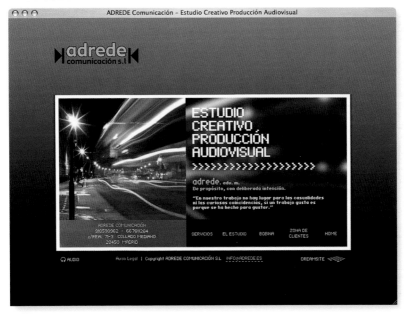

www.adrede.es
D: javier de miguel C: miguel romanillos P: hamadi housami
A: dreamsite M: info@dreamsite.es

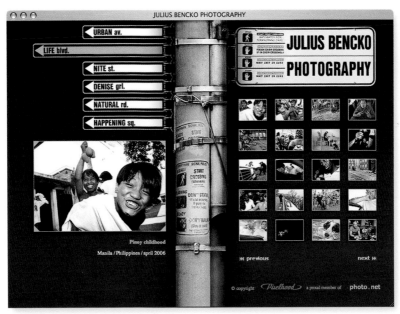

www.juliusbencko.com
D: julius bencko C: julius bencko, alex hajdu P: julius bencko
A: pixelhood twisted designs M: juice@pixelhood.com

oz.dohkoo.com
D: stesha doku C: stesha doku
A: dohkoo M: stesha@dohkoo.com

www.cafelounge.sk
D: michal bartko C: michal bartko
A: webdesignfactory M: michal@webdesignfactory.sk

www.eurosit.com.au
D: michael cathie C: cameron fraser
A: webplace M: www.webplace.com.au

www.lindeloft.com
D: antonello coghe C: antonello coghe P: antonello coghe
A: fashion communication M: antonello@fashionfm.it

www.axelprahl.de
D: stephanie neumann C: stephanie neumann P: stephanie neumann
M: www.werkstadt24.de

www.maximorestaurante.com
D: julio antonio veredas
A: ziddea solutions M: www.ziddea.com

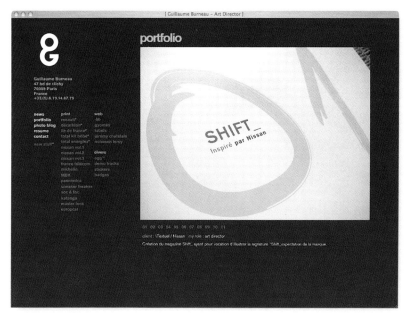

www.gyom80.net
D: guillaume burneau
M: contact@gyom80.net

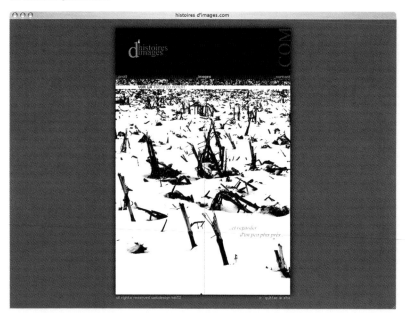

www.histoiresdimages.com
D: yann boudin C: yann boudin P: yann boudin
A: lab52 M: yan@lab52.com

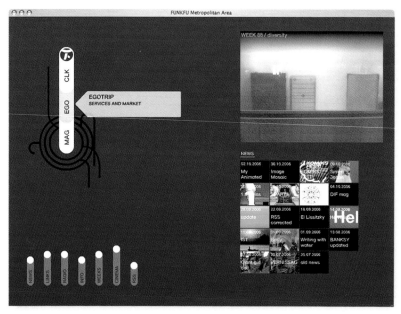

www.funkfu.net
D: martin svoboda C: martin svoboda P: martin svoboda
A: funkfu.net M: www.funkfu.net

www.canusta.com
D: can usta
M: talkto@canusta.com

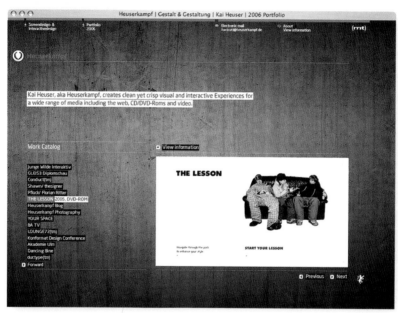

www.heuserkampf.com
D: kai heuser C: kai heuser P: kai heuser
A: heuserkampf M: foxtrott@heuserkampf.de

www.spunkunited.com
D: max hancock
A: fab artificial M: max@spunkunited.com

www.campuscostadelsol.com
D: takeone dsgn
M: tk1@takeone.es

www.vangogh-creative.it
D: enrico penzo C: enrico penzo, luca vinci P: max galli, giorgio guzzi
A: vangogh M: info@vangogh-creative.it

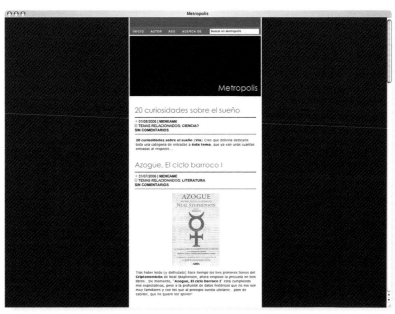

www.niktoprojekt.com/metropolis
D: nikto C: nikto
A: the nikto projekt M: sergiomc@niktoprojekt.com

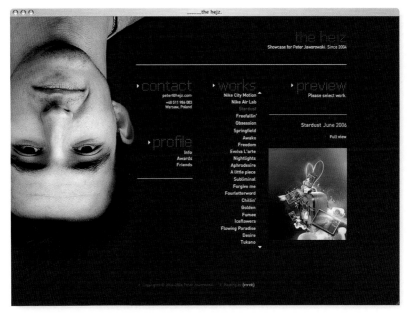

www.hejz.com
D: peter jaworowski C: peter jaworowski P: peter jaworowski
A: the hejz M: peter@hejz.com

www.n-load.com
D: clemens conrad C: holger fitzner
A: n-load.com M: info@n-load.com

mcasd.org/exhibitions/strangenewworld
D: angeles moreno C: angeles moreno P: mcasd, museum of contemporary art san diego
A: www.anaimation.com M: naima@anaimation.com

www.studiobrutus.com
D: lorenzo ceccotti, gianluca abbate, dr. pira C: massimo ronca, mauro staci P: l. ceccotti
A: studio brutus M: info@studiobrutus.com

www.dayseven.co.uk
D: nik jordan
M: still.working@dayseven.co.uk

www.lacrianza.cl
D: fernanda garcia P: maria jesus martorell
A: nuestragencia M: www.nuestragencia.cl

www.strellson.com
D: kay köster, jan peiro C: mario klingemann P: collin croome
A: coma2 e-branding M: collin@coma2.com

www.tdpdesign.com
D: tom painter
A: tdpstudio M: info@tdpdesign.com

www.sessound.com
D: eric lau ching lung C: eric lau ching lung P: eric lau ching lung
A: ericanfly webstudio M: eric@ericanfly.com

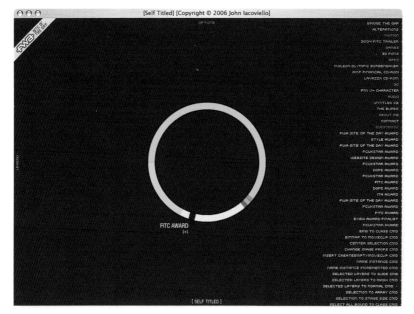

www.selftitled.ca
D: john iacoviello
A: self titled M: john@selftitled.ca

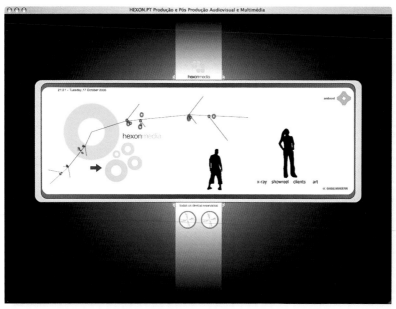

www.hexon.pt
D: nuno pereira C: nuno pereira P: nuno pereira, rute costa
A: hexon M: hexon@hexon.pt

www.gma-la.com
D: kathryn gobright C: kathryn gobright P: kathryn gobright
A: k*motion design M: www.kmotiondesign.com

www.greggy.biz
D: greggy
A: greggy biz M: greggy@greggy.biz

www.alpo.ua
D: darya balova C: sergey kovbasyuk P: alexey kirin
A: ori art group M: www.ori-art.com

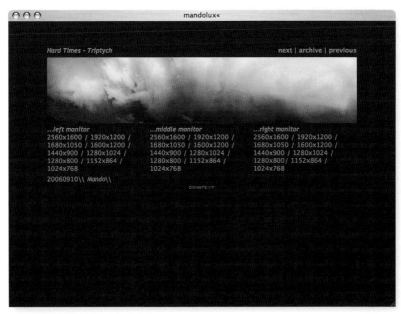

www.mandolux.com
D: mando gomez
A: mandolux M: mando@mandolux.com

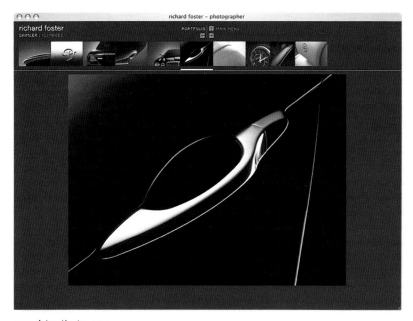

www.richardfoster.com
D: group94 C: group94 P: richard foster
M: info@group94.com

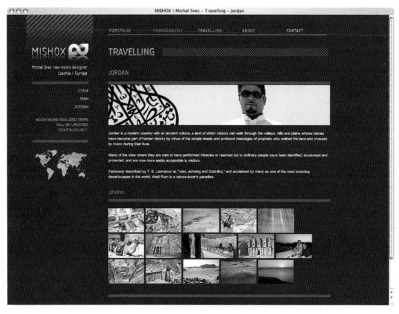

www.mishox.com
D: michal mishox svec C: michal svec P: michal svec
A: mishox new media design M: mishox@mishox.com

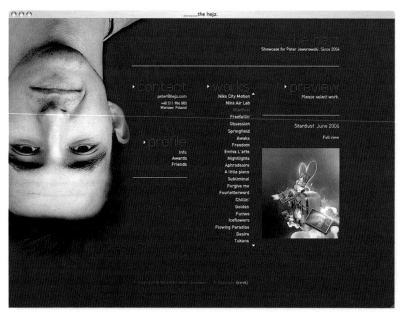

hejz.com
D: peter jaworowski
A: the hejz M: peter@hejz.com

www.cacheila.com
D: a roman, lilliam nieves C: daniel arnaldo roman P: grupo probeta studios
A: grupo probeta studios M: info@grupoprobeta studios

www.davidvana.com
D: samuel gentile C: samuel gentile
A: liquid diamond M: www.liquiddiamond.it

www.sernis.com
D: edigma.com
M: sernis@sernis.com

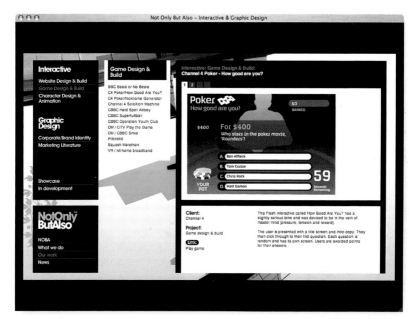

www.notonlybutalso.net
D: steven lester C: dan grant P: nick eakhurst
A: not only but also M: info@notonlybutalso.net

www.chamniseye.com
D: guru design
A: guru design co.,ltd. M: admin@guru-designs.com

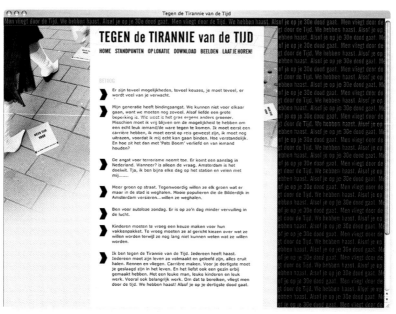

www.tegendetirannievandetijd.nl
D: debby van dongen C: debby van dongen P: debby van dongen
A: conk M: www.conk.nl

www.evicar.it
D: daniele lodi rizzini C: daniele giusti P: daniele lodi rizzini
A: segno&forma M: www.segnoeforma.it

www.forortsungar.se
D: uljana egli C: joakim gullbert
A: lejbrink bennerhult ab M: info@lejbrinkbennerhult.se

www.chilli.be
D: frederik vanderfaeillie C: gaëtan lafaut P: chilli design & multimedia
A: chilli design & multimedia M: info@chilli.be

www.rgbsoul.com
D: pierpaolo balani C: pierpaolo balani P: pierpaolo balani
A: rgb s o u l M: info@rgbsoul.com

www.pakipalmieri.it
D: domenico manno
M: www.manoiki.com

iconfactory.com
D: gedeon maheux, anthony piraino, david lanham C: craig hockenberry
A: the iconfactory M: iconfactory.com/home/contact

bossatonika.com
D: luis giraldez, clara rojas C: luis giraldez P: luis giraldez
A: guiro.net M: luis@guiro.net

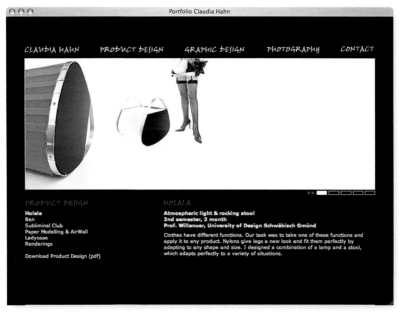

www.inthepink.de
D: claudia hahn, joe landen C: claudia hahn, joe landen P: claudia hahn, joe landen
A: twinpix web.print.music M: info@twinpix.de

www.fenabel.com
D: paula granja C: paula granja P: paula granja
A: pcw M: paulagranja@pcw.pt

www.ig-hk.com
D: pippen lau C: pippen lau P: pippen lau
A: intermedia group M: it@ig-hk.com

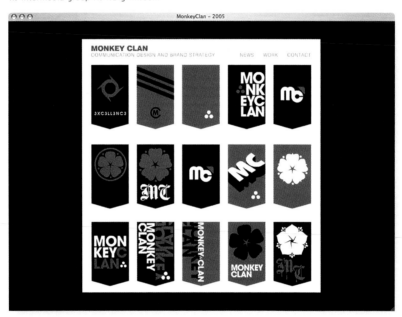

www.monkeyclan.com
D: kai pham C: atul ohri, jon rubino P: angelo fabara
A: monkey clan M: info@monkeyclan.com

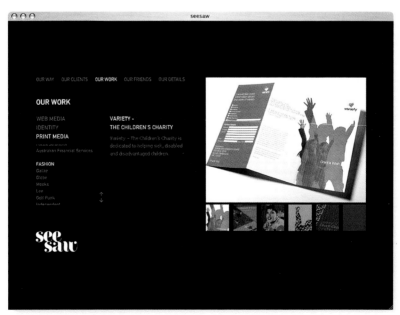

www.seesawdesign.com.au
D: seesaw design C: gaby garcia P: sam pascua
A: 4pd M: info@4pd.com.au

www.deangelisarch.com
D: ivan pedri C: ivan pedri P: ivan pedri
A: deangelis architetti M: info@geturl.it

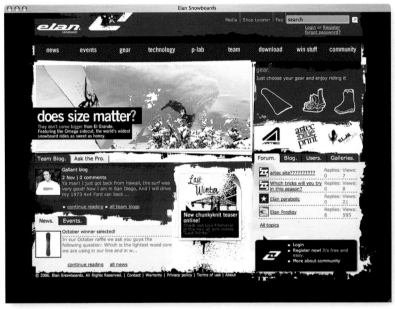

www.elansnowboards.com
D: gregor zakelj C: bojan mihelac P: gregor zakelj
A: subtotal M: www.subtotal.nu

www.neuerepublika.com
D: áthila armstrong C: leonardo oliveira P: leonardo oliveira
A: neuerepublika M: armstrong@neuerepublika.com

www.didoo.net
D: cristiano rastelli C: cristiano rastelli
A: area web M: public@didoo.net

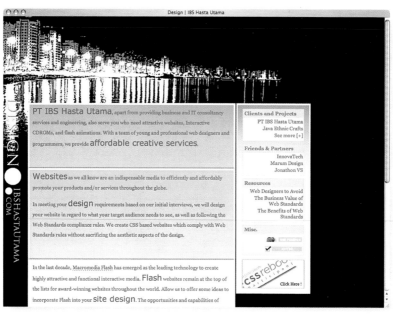

design.ibshastautama.com
D: anggie bratadinata
A: pt ibs hasta utama M: mas_ab@ibshastautama.com

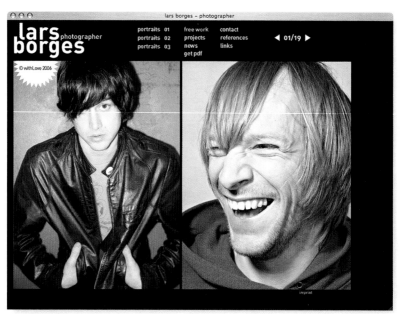

www.larsborges.de
D: lars borges, lisa schibel C: lars borges P: lars borges
A: lars borges M: hey@larsborges.de

www.liquisoft.com
D: ryan ford C: ryan ford
M: rford@liquisoft.com

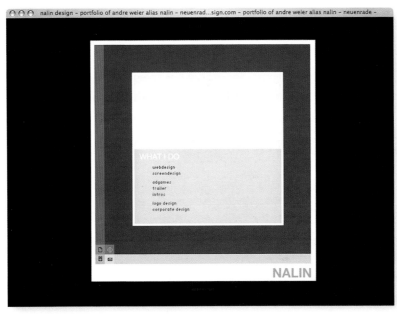

www.nalindesign.com
D: andre weier C: andre weier P: andre weier
A: nalindesign M: info@nalindesign.com

www.3pointsblue.com
D: art johnson, marketa sadkova C: marketa sadkova P: art johnson
A: wired hand M: art@3pointsblue.com

www.schernelz-village.ch
D: serge rau C: mehmet ayas P: orange8 interactive ag
A: orange8 interactive ag M: serge.rau@orange8.com

www.ctdia.com.br/hotsite
D: bruno piza, rafael paiva C: fábio lonardoni, rafael ribeiro P: fabiano cruz
A: opusmúltipla M: web@opusmultipla.com.br

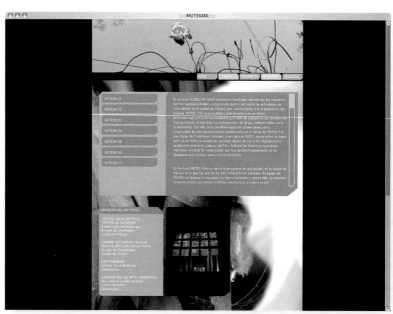

www.strobe.com.mx/mutek/
D: alexis yasky, rodrigo tovar C: flash corp. P: damian romero
A: sociedad anonima M: contacto@sociedadanonima.info

www.prodigomultimedia.net
D: francisco gómez C: francisco gómez P: francisco gómez
A: prodigo multimedia M: info@prodigomultimedia.net

www.katharinahesse.com
D: lili xue, beijing, china C: g2 studio, hongkong P: katharina hesse
M: kathchina@yahoo.de

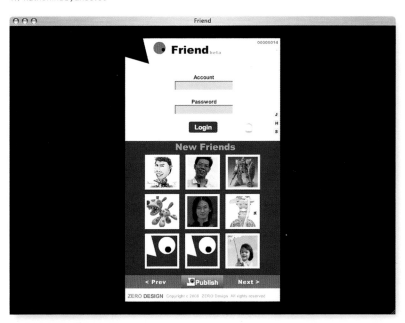

www.3zero.com/friend
D: zero C: friend P: zero
A: zero M: www.3zero.com

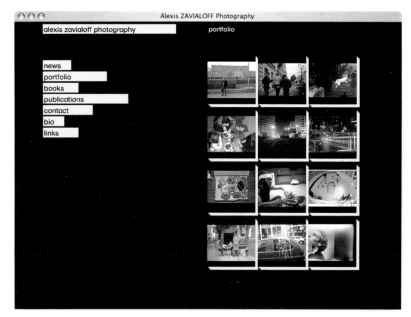

www.souledhere.com
D: martin svoboda C: martin svoboda P: alexis zavialoff
A: www.funkfu.net M: az@souledhere.com

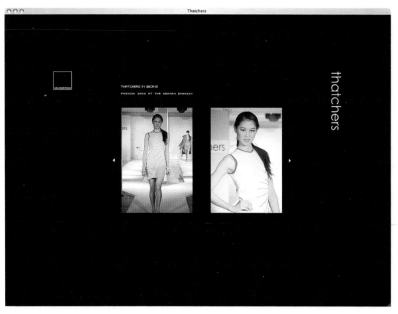

www.thatchers.de
D: ralf hensellek C: thomas mrozek
A: thatchers hensellek, mrozek M: ilovestyle@thatchers.de

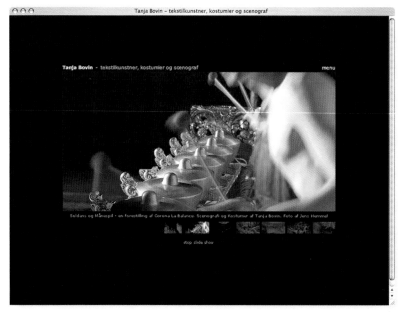

www.tanjabovin.dk
D: lars bregendahl bro C: lars bregendahl bro P: lars bregendahl bro
A: westend.dk M: www.westend.dk

www.fishouse.net
D: alessandro orlandi
A: fishouse M: ask@somnianti

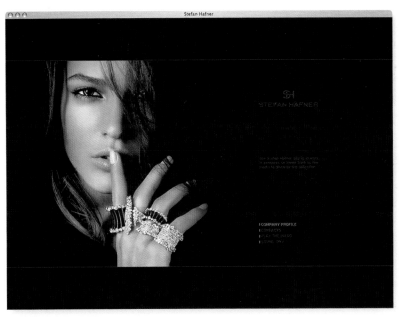

www.stefanhafner.com
D: caroline hue C: dynamic foundry staff P: dynamic foundry staff
A: dynamic foundry M: caroline.hue@dynamicfoundry.com

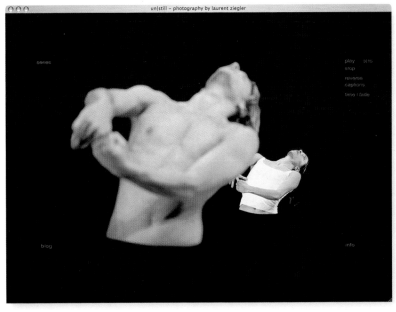

www.unstill.net
D: laurent ziegler, helmut prochart C: helmut prochart P: laurent ziegler
A: sitedefinition M: info@sitedefinition.at

www.dysplasii.com
D: emmanuel prissette
M: contact@dysplasii.com

www.mobilirenzobianchi.it
D: alessio papi
A: success multimedia company M: www.success.it

```
○○○                           Acconci Studio
Acconci Studio  20 Jay St. Suite #215, Brooklyn, NY 11201  Tel: 718.852.6591 Fax: 718.624.3178  e-mail: studio@acconci.com

1 1991 1992 1993 1995 1996 1997 1998 1999 2 2000 2001 2002 2003 2004 2005
A Adjustable-Adaptable-Convertible Airports Anyang Linear Building Atlanta Airport Transfer Corridors Atria
Austin Water Park Austria B Bend-Fold Braid-Knot-Weave Brazil Breda Garbage Dump Bridges Buildings
Built Bulge-Bubble-Ooze C Cambridge Bus Shelter Canada Capsules Car Hotel Celia Imrey Circle-Spiral
Circulation Routes Clusters Coffee And Tea Set Container Continuous Surface-Endless Space
Courtyard In The Wind D Darío Núñez Display-Exhibition Design E Eduardo Marques England
Expanding-Contracting Eyebeam Modular Lounge F Facade Flourescent Furniture Flying-Floating France
Fulton Street Atrium G Gallery-Museum Garbage-Waste Garrett Ricciardi Germany Gia Wolff
Grains-Particles-Bits Guadalajara Library Gurtel Median Park H Hiriya Garbage Dump Hotels
House Up A Building I In Development Inside-Out Interiors Islands Israel Italy J Japan K Klapper Hall Plaza
Klein Bottle Playground Korea L Lights London New Street Square Loop Luis Vera M MAK Design Store
Marienhof Plaza Markets Memphis Performing Arts Center Plaza MetroTech Garden Mexico Milan Facade
Mix-Swarm-Multitude Mobile Linear City Modules Move-Change Mur Island Möbius Bench N Netherlands
New World Trade Center New York City Lights Novartis Park And Parking P Parasite-Virus Park In The Water
Park Up A Building Parking Parks and Gardens Personal Island Peter Dorsey Philadelphia Airport Flying Floors
Playgrounds Portables-Vehicles Pratt Display System Prototype Publications Puerto Rico Push and Pull
Q Queens Museum Renovation R Reflective Replication-Multiplication-Proliferation Restaurants
Rome Sound Museum Rotate-Revolve S Saks Fifth Avenue Windows San Juan Skate Park
Sao Paulo Highway House And Garden Sarina Basta Schachter ConTEMPorary Scottsdale Transportation Center
Screen-Overlay-Camouflage Seating Sehzat Oner Seoul Performing Arts Center Services Shelters
Shibuya Station Shift-Pivot Sky Sound Sound Shell Spain Spheres-Globes-Worlds
Split-Separate-Strips and Strands Stephen Roe Storefront For Art And Architecture Stores Strasbourg Plaza
Streets and Plazas Stretch-Overlap-Tentacles and Feelers Switzerland T Tele-Furni System Telescoping
Theaters Theoretical Theoretical Gallery Toronto Waterpark City Perimeter Transparent-Translucent
Transportation Tube-Tunnel-Funnel Twist-Warp-Morph U Umbruffla Unbuilt United Bamboo Store
United States V Video Vito Acconci W W 8th Street Subway Station Watersides-Outlands Wave-Ripple-Flow
Wind World In Your Bones Wrap
```

www.acconci.com
D: eric rodenbeck P: eric rodenbeck
A: stamen design M: studio@acconci.com

336

www.lutoslawski-duo.com
D: mikolaj sadowski C: mikolaj sadowski P: mikolaj sadowski
A: sadowski interactive M: m.sadowski@sinteractive.eu

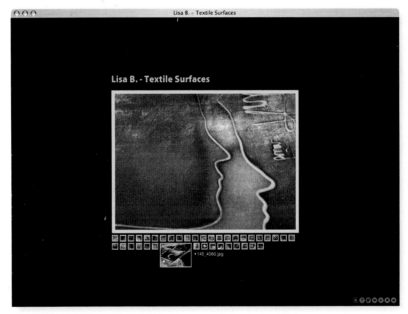

www.lisabaeck.com
D: dietmar halbauer, roman drahosz C: roman drahosz P: embers consulting
A: embers consulting M: d.halbauer@embers.at

www.omniwear.com
D: ricardo ferreira C: ricardo ferreira P: eduardo freitas
A: omni M: omni@omniwear.com

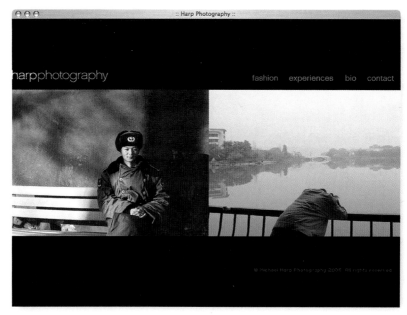

www.harpphotography.com
D: brennan boblett
A: brennan boblett designs M: michael@harpphotography.com

www.visualo.de/artsite2
D: norbert coors C: norbert coors P: norbert coors
A: visualo.de M: visualo@visualo.de

www.gaeaulenti.it
D: fabio, dario zannier C: caroline hue, dario cappa, rocco trombetta
A: indaco sas, dynamic foundry M: caroline.hue@dynamicfoundry.com

www.marsigliocar.it
D: marcello vigoni C: marcello vigoni P: carrozzeria marsiglio
A: tuninglove services snc M: www.tl-services.com

www.ristorantegiapponese.com
D: giovanni paletta C: giovanni paletta P: giovanni paletta
A: krghettojuice.com M: krghettojuice@hotmail.com

www.33restaurant.com/lounge
D: david ghelman
A: the inet group M: info@inetgroup.com

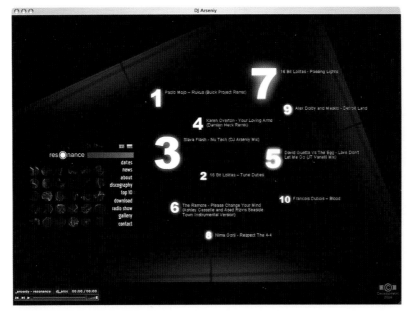

resonance.com.ua
D: nicolov a. C: xorbit P: igor t. brovco
A: advertising agency cybota M: mail@cybota.com

www.suspiciousminds.com
D: reginald van de velde C: reginald van de velde P: reginald van de velde
A: suspiciousminds M: lenzz@yucom.be

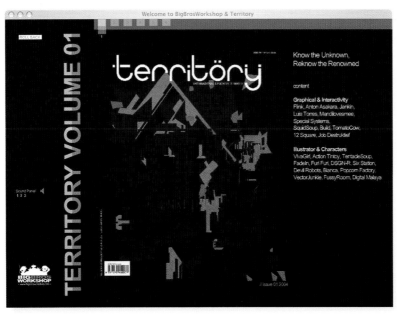

www.bigbrosworkshop.com
D: simon so
A: vector bros studio M: simon@vectorbros.com

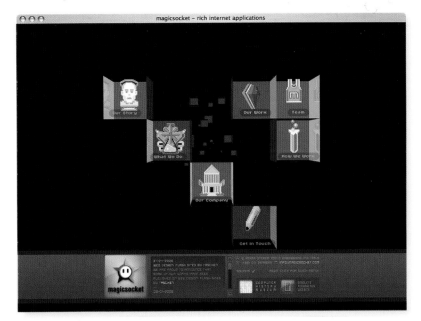

www.magicsocket.com
D: marco corti, mario ballario
A: magicsocket s.r.l. M: info@magicsocket.com

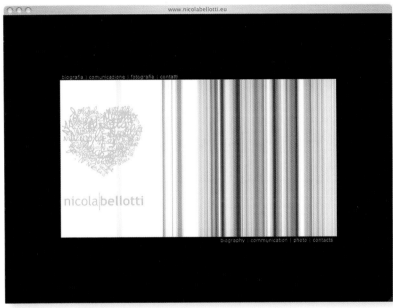

www.nicolabellotti.eu
D: nicola bellotti C: nicola bellotti P: ghita pasquali
A: blacklemon M: g.pasquali@blacklemon.com

www.hydra-newmedia.com
D: daniel gebhard C: markus heckel P: martin eymer, frank pomereinke
A: hydra newmedia. stuttgart M: contact@hydra-newmedia.com

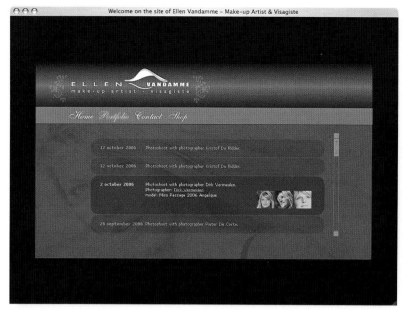

www.ellenvandamme.be
D: lore deroo C: gwen vanhee P: meridian
A: meridian M: www.meridian.be

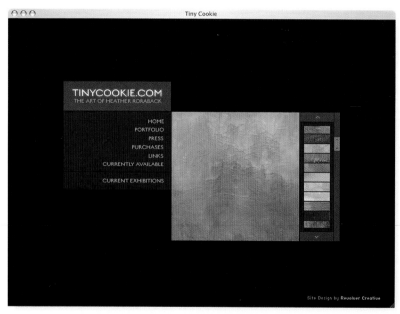

www.tinycookie.com
D: matthew fordham
A: revolver creative M: www.revolvercreative.com

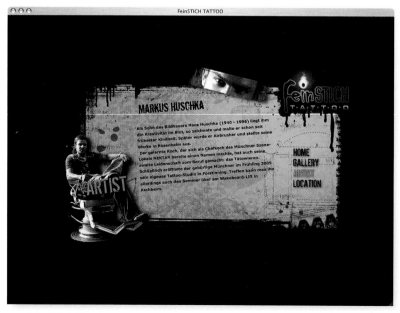

www.feinstich-tattoo.de
D: karsten sondersorg C: stefan schröder
M: info@feinstich-tattoo.de

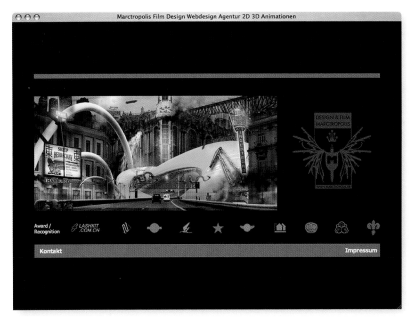

www.marctropolis.de
D: marc fehse C: chris heyder P: marc fehse
A: marctropolis M: marc@marctropolis.de

www.nunohorta.com
D: nuno horta
A: nhdesign M: geral@nunohorta.com

www.addictedflavours.com
D: becker sven C: gilles dumont P: bitmap s.à.r.l., addicted flavours
A: bitmap s.à.r.l. M: sven@bitmap.lu

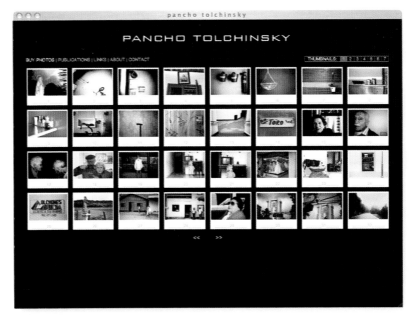

www.pilsjart.com
D: pancho tolchinsky
M: tolchinsky@gmail.com

www.norrb.com
D: pawel nolbert
A: norrb.com M: paul@norrb.com

www.insert.gr
D: stamatios sarris C: stamatios sarris P: stamatios sarris
A: insert M: insert@insert.gr

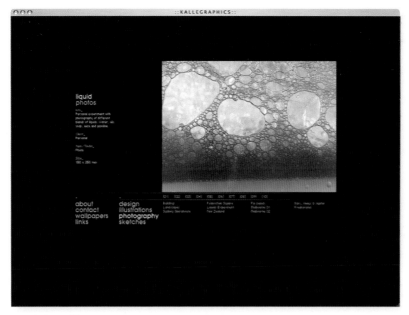

www.kallegraphics.com
D: karl martin sætren C: karl martin sætren P: karl martin sætren
A: kallegraphics M: email@kallegraphics.com

www.defasten.com
D: patrick doan
A: defasten M: info@defasten.com

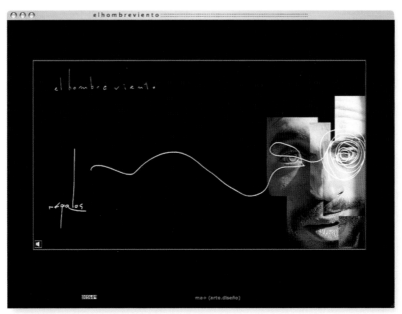

www.elhombreviento.com
D: maite camacho C: mario gutiérrez P: jeremías pau toledo
A: ma+ (arte.diseño) M: info@estudiomamas.com

www.markpipher.com
D: mark pipher
M: mark@markpipher.com

www.asemota.de
D: stefan asemota
M: stefan@asemota.de

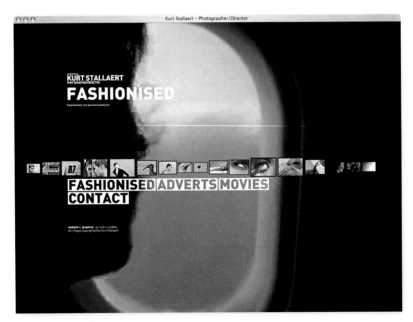

www.kurtstallaert.be
D: milk and cookies C: milk and cookies P: milk and cookies
A: kurt stallaert M: kurt@kurtstallaert.be

www.ianwharton.com
D: ian wharton
M: an@ianwharton.com

discoapp.com
D: japser hauser
A: discoapp.com M: info@madebysofa.com

www.rarz.net
D: jericó santander cabrera C: jericó santander cabrera P: jericó santander cabrera
A: taller de ideas atutiplen M: jericosantander@gmail.com

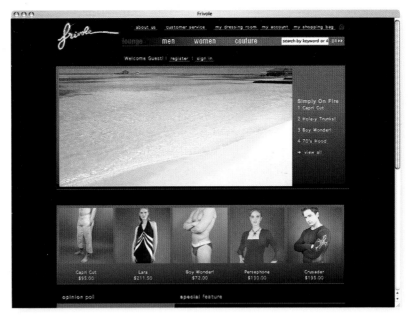

www.frivole.com
D: breathewords.com
M: www.breathewords.com

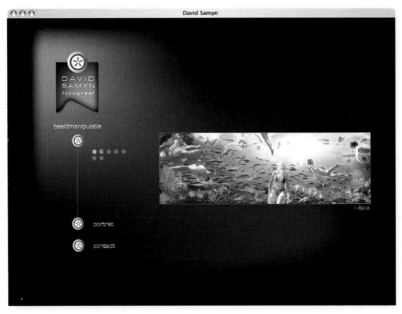

www.davidsamyn.be/
D: frederik fonteyne C: hans van de velde P: david samyn
A: frederik fonteyne M: hans@novio.be

www.gbaggio.com
D: grzegorz badzio C: blazej wocial P: grzegorz badzio
A: grzegorz badzio fine art photography M: gb@gbaggio.com

www.ralfwenkerstyling.de
D: andreas hagemann C: oliver soecknick P: andreas hagemann
A: hagemannplus M: www.hagemannplus.de

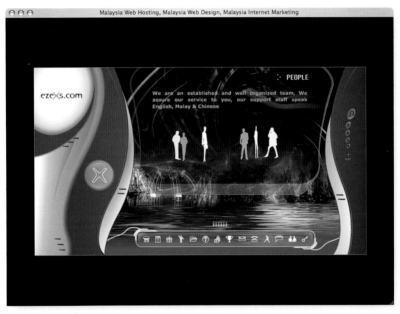

www.ezexs.com/index2.html
D: henry yap C: henry yap P: henry yap
A: easy access interactive management M: henryap@gmail.com

www.flashcreativa.com
D: antonio rivera páez C: antonio rivera P: antonio rivera
A: flashcreativa estudios M: rivera@flashcreativa.com

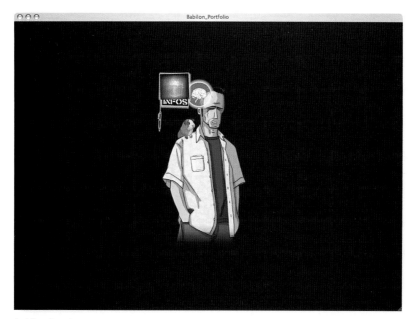

babilon.free.fr
D: babilon romain
M: babilon@free.fr

www.twocreate.co.uk
D: sam dallyn C: brendan lynch P: sam dallyn
A: two create M: info@twocreate.co.uk

www.omkamra.hu/tulsoketetes
D: ctrlfreak, mindcycled C: dr.zsoci P: vidéki béla
A: fekete jéé, omkamra M: ctrlfreak@chello.hu

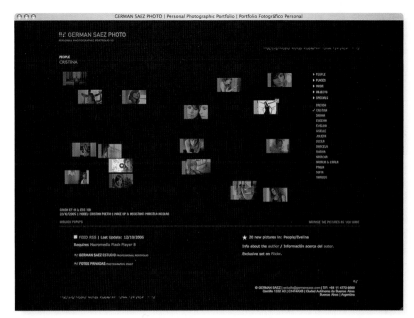

germansaezphoto.com
D: germán saez
A: germán saez estudio M: germansaezphoto.com

www.throw2catch.com
D: philippe roy C: philippe roy
A: 1l 2p M: phil@unldeuxp.com

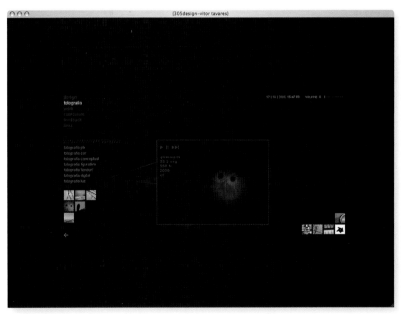

www.305design.net
D: vitor tavares C: vitor tavares P: © 305design, vitor tavares
A: 305design studio M: vitor.tavares@305design.net, vitor.tavares@caetsu.pt

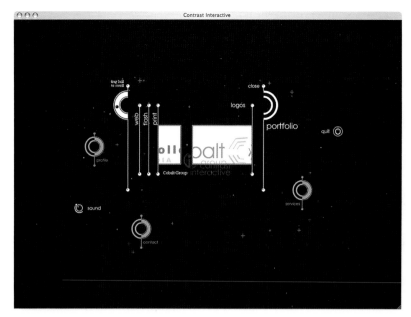

www.contrast-interactive.com
D: alexander brener C: alexander brener P: alexander brener
A: contrast interactive M: brener@contrast-interactive.com

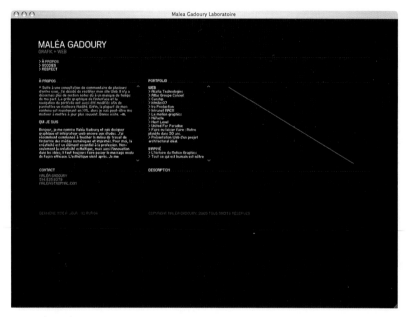

www.maleagadoury.com
D: maléa gadoury
M: malea@tropmal.com

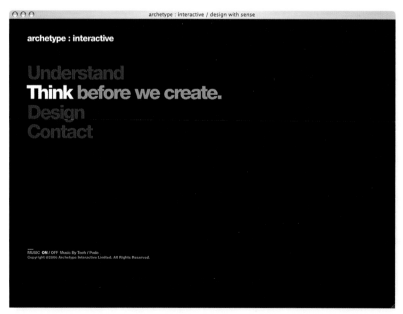

www.a-i.com.hk
D: john wu, dick po C: yeson ye P: john wu
A: archetype interactive limited M: info@a-i.com.hk

index of designers

index of designers

index of designers

index of designers

index of designers

index of designers

index of designers

index of designers

index of designers

index of designers

index of URLs

index of URLs

index of URLs

index of URLs

index of URLs

index of URLs